IMAGES
of America

DOOR COUNTY

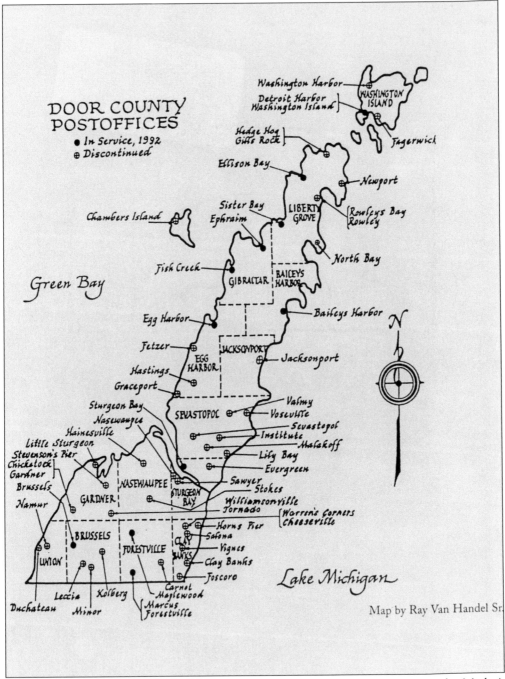

This is a map by Ray Van Handel Sr. Reprinted with permission from "Going for the Mail: A History of Door County's Post Offices," by James B. Hale.

IMAGES
of America

DOOR
COUNTY

Joseph W. Zurawski

ARCADIA

Published by Arcadia Publishing,
an imprint of Tempus Publishing, Inc.
2 Cumberland Street
Charleston, SC 29401

Printed in Great Britain.

Library of Congress Catalog Card Number: 98-87137

For all general information contact Arcadia Publishing at:
Telephone 843-853-2070
Fax 843-853-0044
E-Mail arcadia@charleston.net

For customer service and orders:
Toll-Free 1-888-313-BOOK

Visit us on the internet at http://www.arcadiaimages.com

CONTENTS

Acknowledgments   6

Introduction   7

1.   Early Settlements   9

2.   Economic Life   21

3.   Ships and Shipbuilding   59

4.   Religion   75

5.   Education   91

6.   Resorts   97

7.   Cultural and Social Life   111

ACKNOWLEDGMENTS

I would like to thank the following individuals who have shared their knowledge, photographs, and enthusiasm about Door County and its significant history with me. Without their assistance, this work could not have been completed.

Mary Reynolds Aiken, Sandy Andre, Dan Austad, Bill Bastian, Goodwin Berquist (Washington Island Archives), Thomas Blackwood (Peninsula State Park), Rev. Kenneth Boettcher, Fritz Brunswilk, Harry (Sr.) and Hazel Chaudoir, Bill and Fran Cecil, Nancy Emery (Sturgeon Bay Library), John Enigl Sr., Allen Erickson, George Evenson (Sturgeon Bay Historical Association), Christine Falk-Pederson (Gibraltar Bay Historical Association), Wallace Felhofer (Door County Museum), Jon Gast, Rev. Patrick Gawrylewski, Gretle and Bill Goettelman, Bill Graf, Rev. Paul Graf, Stephen R. Grutzmacher, James B. Hale, James Halstead Sr. (Jacksonport Historical Association), Gloria Hansen, Rev. Marge Hassler, Sally Jacobson (Ephraim Foundation), Marie Hein (Jacksonport Historical Society), Ann Jankins (Door County Historical Museum), Eva Kita, Eldred Koepsel, Rev. Matthew Knapp, William G. Laatsch, June Larsen (Door County Maritime Museum), M. Marvin Lotz, Catherine and Jeanette McArdle, Rev. Bill Patterson, Annie Peil, Leonard Peterson, Paul Regnier, Howard Renard, Dick Purinton, Christine Randall (Door County Maritime Museum), Eunice Rutherford, Orv Schopf, Roger Schroeder, Bill Skadden, Gary Soule, Rev. Randall Styx, Marilyn Vandertie, and Mary Wilson.

My appreciation is also extended to Patrick Catel of Arcadia Publishing, who was most receptive to the idea of this work and helped guide me through its publication.

INTRODUCTION

Keeping the four fingers of your left hand together and the tip of your thumb an inch away, place your hand flat. You are now looking at the state of Wisconsin, and the thumb is the 90-mile peninsula that is today's Door County.

Increase Claflin is generally acknowledged as the first permanent white settler on the Door peninsula. He purchased land from the federal government in Green Bay and built a log cabin trading post in 1835 in an area near today's Little Sturgeon Bay. In 1848, Captain Justin Bailey, while bound for Milwaukee with a cargo that included immigrants, ran into a violent storm. Bailey found his way to the first available harbor. Strong winds continued for several days. The crew and several passengers were able to get ashore. They found rock that could be quarried and timber suitable for cord wood. Bailey reported these findings to Alanson Sweet, a Milwaukee financier who owned ships that sailed on Lake Michigan. A village was set up in 1849, and the following year a stack of cord wood measuring 20,000 feet long, 10,000 feet wide, and 10,000 feet high was shipped from Baileys Harbor.

Sturgeon Bay began to emerge as a major commercial center after the first of three commercial sawmills was built in 1853. A newspaper, the *Door County Advocate*, which is still published today, was launched in 1862. The early village was called Graham, then Tehema, and, in 1860, Sturgeon Bay.

The period after the Civil War saw dramatic changes influencing the economy of the Door peninsula. Lumber was in great demand, as numerous railroads needed millions of ties for the tracks they were laying. Chicago, particularly after the fire of 1871, and other cities needed large amounts of lumber for housing. As the land was cleared in the Door peninsula, farms sprang up. Wheat and other grains were grown. Dairy products increased farm income. A market for wool developed around the turn of the century. Strawberries, peaches, pears, plums, and cranberries were grown in the area. Despite this initial variety, apple and cherry trees were to dominate Door's landscape well into the 20th century.

Joseph Zettel had a farm north of Sturgeon Bay. Following meetings with the College of Agriculture at the University of Wisconsin, Zettel planted a 45-acre apple orchard. Eventually, he was harvesting 3,000 bushels annually. In 1893, his apples received highly favorable comments after they were displayed in Chicago during the World Fair's Columbian Exposition.

Other industries had degrees of success in Door County. The fishing industry was a prosperous business for many years. Sturgeon were plentiful until the Sturgeon Bay Canal opened in 1881. There were also quarries in Sturgeon Bay, Ephraim, Baileys Harbor, and

Washington Island. Ice harvesting provided hundreds of tons of ice which were shipped from Sturgeon Bay to Chicago between 1870 and 1900.

Shipbuilding was the peninsula's major industry for many years. August Riebolt and Joseph Wolter bought a site in Sturgeon Bay which they eventually opened in 1906 as the Universal Shipbuilding Company. Later it became Sturgeon Bay Dry Dock Company. By 1917, it was the largest single commercial business on the peninsula. The firm of Leathem and Smith was building tugboats during World War I and eventually employed 5,000 workers. Martin Peterson opened Peterson Boat Works in 1908, but it was not until the 1930s that the firm prospered. It was awarded several naval contracts during World War II. Palmer Johnson began as a firm specializing in the building and repair of fishing vessels. The focus of its business changed somewhat, and after 1928 the firm was building yachts for customers all over the world.

Comprehensive figures have not been compiled that would reflect the hundreds of millions of visitors, tourists, vacationers, and campers to the Door peninsula over the years. In the 1920s, major steamship companies brought hundreds of passengers per boat load that would dock at the piers of the peninsula. For a while, a daily bus service ran between Green Bay and Sturgeon Bay. In 1923, it was estimated some 500,000 visited Door County. Since that time, that number has more than quadrupled on an annual basis, with many visiting throughout the year rather than only in the summer months, as was the practice earlier in the century.

Religious, cultural, and social activities in Door County have been greatly influenced by the influx of visitors. Churches were built, rebuilt, and expanded, often with a view of accommodating visitors. Major institutions, such as the Peninsula Players, were launched to provide a welcome haven for avid theater professionals and fans. The Clearing encouraged students of architecture as well as other fine arts. The Ridges Sanctuary occupies 1,200 acres, where some 428 flowering plants have been identified, as well as 347 non-flowering shoots. It was designated a national landmark by the United States Department of the Interior, and was the first such area in Wisconsin to be so designated.

Close to 95 percent of the area of Door County remains non-commercial. Visitors, encouraged by extensive publicity campaigns, continue to flock to the area. Even though every summer weekend has some type of festival or special event which attracts upwards of 100,000 people, the area continues to retain its small-town atmosphere. In fact, there are only two major highways, both two-lane, and no green electric traffic signals north of Sturgeon Bay. This book represents a glimpse into the history of the unique area that is Door County.

One

EARLY SETTLEMENTS

Although individual white settlers came to the Door Peninsula in the 1830s—Increase Claflin near Sturgeon Bay and Amos Lovejoy on Rock Island—the first established community was at Ephraim. A founding stone (above right) was dedicated in 1923. It reads as follows: "Near this spot a Moravian congregation, Rev. A.M. Iverson, Pastor, landed in May, 1853 forming the first permanent colony in Door County." The photo above was taken around 1915 and shows the Bethany Lutheran Church on the left, the old Anderson Hotel, and the Hillside Hotel on the right. (Courtesy of Mary Wilson.)

Here is early Ephraim as it appears in a painting by Rev. A.M. Iverson in 1859. The Ephraim Moravian Church, which Reverend Iverson founded, is on the right side of the painting. Reverend Iverson is also credited with the founding of Ephraim in 1853, when a congregation, led by Reverend Iverson, purchased 424.75 acres for $478, according to his proposed Eagle Bay Plan. He and his followers moved from Green Bay to the present site of Ephraim, although the congregation decided to call their new home Ephraim ("doubly fruitful") before they made their move. After they arrived and built modest dwellings, the settlement was often referred to as "Shantytown."

The Goodletson cabin was built by Thomas Goodletson in 1848–50 on Horseshoe Island, which is near Ephraim. During the 1860s it was slid across the ice to the area occupied today by the Ephraim condominiums. Meetings of the Bethany Lutheran Church were conducted in the cabin until a church was built for the congregation in the 1880s. In 1974 the cabin was given to the Ephraim Foundation, which has maintained the cabin. The original part of the cabin was moved to its present site on a hillside near the Bethany Lutheran Church. Artifacts from the 1850s are on display when the cabin is open during the summer season.

Here is Ephraim as it appeared about 100 years ago. This view is looking north from the merger of today's Highway 42 and Moravia Road, branching off to the right. (Courtesy of Allen Erickson.)

This is the view looking south from the north end of current Highway 42 in Ephraim, around 1900. The road extends to the site of present-day Wilson Schaefer Real Estate, and in the foreground would be the area of today's Waterbury and Blue Dolphin. (Courtesy of Mary Wilson.)

The Anderson dock in Ephraim was built in the late 1850s by Aslag Anderson. By the early 1870s, Anderson's dock was being used to ship off hundreds of shipments of wood to markets in Chicago, Milwaukee, and other destinations. Thanks to his business agreements, Anderson also arranged for wood to be shipped from other piers on the Door peninsula. (Courtesy of Henry A. Anderson, M.D.)

This panoramic view of Ephraim was taken around 1920. Eagle Island is in the distance on the right. The Hillside Hotel is in the lower left. The building in the background on the left is no longer standing. It is across the street from Wilson Ice Cream, which was opened in 1906. Oscar Wilson's residence is in the center foreground. (Courtesy of Mary Wilson.)

Little Sister Bay was developed around 1857. A pier was built to accommodate ships that hauled lumber products from the nearby forests. There was also a store, a blacksmith shop, and a saloon. A ship arrived in 1865 with a crew suffering from diphtheria. All died except one crew member. There was concern that the disease might spread. A sheep pasture was quickly converted into a cemetery. After that incident, Little Sister Bay declined in importance while Sister Bay, under the leadership of Andre Seaquist, emerged as a village. When the above photo was taken, probably around 1900, the old fish house on Little Sister Bay had little business. (Courtesy of Allen Erickson.)

The main street in Sister Bay is pictured here in 1908, near the intersection of present-day Highways 42 and ZZ. The building in the center, Koepsel's dance hall, is today's Sister Bay Bowl. The building on the right was the private residence of Casper Nyes, with a dental office upstairs along with a barbershop owned by Bill Burns. Since 1952 the site has been the Village View Motel. (Courtesy of the Door County Museum.)

Here is the view looking south on what was to become Highway 42 in Sister Bay at the turn of the century. The Ole Erickson store is the large building on the right. It was a general store until Carl Benson purchased the property and opened a small furniture store. It was then Witalison's Furniture, Wilke Furniture, and today is the site of Al Johnson's shop, across the street from his restaurant. Joe Hendrickson's garage was near the top of the road on the right (now Husby's), across the street from today's Sister Bay Bowl on the left of the street. (Courtesy of Allen Erickson.)

An Olsen family portrait is shown here at their settlement around 1876, in the Fish Creek area that was later to become the Nicolet Bay Campground and the State Game Farm in Peninsula State Park. (Courtesy of Peninsula State Park Archives.)

14

This is the view from today's Irish House in Fish Creek looking south on what was then Highway 17 (today's Highway 42). The Irish House was constructed from a boat and moved to the present location. Apflebach's barn is shown in the center of this early-1900s photo. (Courtesy Gibraltar Historical Association.)

Baileys Harbor, pictured here in the early 1900s, shows Preuter's Flour and Saw Mill on the left. The building in the center is the site of the present-day Yum-Yum Tree. The view is from Bluff Road looking east. On the right is the site of the present-day Blue Ox, and the tall building in the background is occupied by Florian II today. (Courtesy of Immanuel Lutheran Church Archives.)

In the early years of the 20th century, this photo was taken from the German Lutheran Church in Baileys Harbor. The church in the photo is St. Mary of The Lake. Baileys Harbor schoolhouse appears near the steeple. The large building on the right is today's Frontier Bar and Restaurant. (Courtesy of Immanuel Lutheran Church Archives.)

Baileys Harbor is pictured here around 1905. This view is looking south on Highway 78 (today's 57). August Schramm's Dance Hall, today's Frontier Bar, is on the left. Note the wooden sidewalks with handrails. (Courtesy of Allen Erickson.)

This is a view of Egg Harbor looking south around 1900. The Cupola House, a National Historic Landmark, is on the left. To the right of the Cupola House was Dolly's Ice Cream Parlor, today's Hideside. Continuing right is the old schoolhouse, Levi Thorp's hardware store, and Casey's, which is still managed today as a restaurant. (Courtesy of Gloria Hansen.)

A view of Ellison Bay is seen here in the early years of the 20th century. Trinity Lutheran Church can be seen on the right in the background. The large building in front of the church is the Hillside, which was a popular spot for many dances in the early decades of the 20th century. (Courtesy of Allen Erickson.)

Ellison Bay is pictured here in the early years of the 20th century. Charlie Ruckert's general store (today's Pioneer Store) is on the left, and the schoolhouse is on the right. Gus Klenky's garage is in the center, and the building right next to the road was Louis J. Neman's hotel. That building was constructed during the 1880s and has served as a general store, an implement store, a dentist's office, a private residence, a bookstore, an art gallery, and today serves as Gills Rock Stoneware of Ellison Bay. (Courtesy of Allen Erickson.)

Several Ellison Bay postal cards in the first decade of the 20th century attempted to portray how "modern" Ellison Bay was by showing a streetcar on tracks. They were probably responding to similar cards promoting other areas of the county at that time. Note the "additional" utility pole in front of the store on the left. In Sturgeon Bay, a "vintage" Orville and Wilbur Wright airplane was shown hovering above one of the main streets around 1910. (Courtesy of Allen Erickson.)

Here is a street scene in Jacksonport looking south around 1910. The J.A. La Mere general store, built in 1885, is on the left, in an area occupied by the Square Rigger Lodge today. Charlie Reynold's store is in the center on the left of the road. Reynolds moved to Jacksonport in 1876 and reportedly sold large quantities of goods. He was also in the lumber and forest products business with annual revenues of $25,000. His building became Carmody's Grocery Store. Thomas Reynolds, the brother of Charlie, became a Wisconsin assemblyman. Thomas's son, John, became attorney general, and his grandson, John, became Wisconsin's governor. (Courtesy of Allen Erickson.)

An aerial view of Rowleys Bay in the 1930s suggests what the area looked like in the early 1870s. In 1870, 1,500 cords of wood, 6,000 railroad ties, 8,000 telegraph poles, and 60,000 cedar posts were shipped from Rowleys Bay. The following year the shipments included 16,000 telegraph poles, 60,000 cedar posts, 6,000 ties, and 15,000 cords of wood. (Courtesy of Leonard Peterson.)

The area of Gill's Rock has a rather dynamic history in the second half of the 19th century. Elias Gill, a timber operator and pier owner, cleared some 1,300 acres. A stone quarry, north of Gill's Rock, after a flurry of activity in the 1850s, finally closed. In 1882, the Newhall House burned and 180 guests perished. By 1900 the area was no longer a hub of activity, and the post office was closed in 1904. Most residents who remained continued, or turned to, fishing. (Courtesy of Door County Maritime Museum.)

An "Irish Village" sprung up on the west side of Washington Harbor on Washington Island around 1900. Approximately 12 families struggled to preserve their cultural identity while fishing and farming. The settlement was abandoned in the 1930s. An African-American colony of similar size also existed on Washington Island but was abandoned after a few years. (Courtesy of Washington Island Archives.)

Two

ECONOMIC LIFE

Logging became an important activity in Jacksonport in 1867 when a logging camp and two piers were built. A crew of 37 woodchoppers cut their way from Sturgeon Bay to Jacksonport. Within a year they loaded 80 ships with cedar posts, railroad ties, telegraph poles, and cord wood. By the 1880s the amount of trees available for logging was greatly reduced in the Jacksonport area and people began leaving the village. It was reported that some 852 left Jacksonport in 1882. The lumber business gave way to farming and cord wood production. The above photo, taken around 1910 in Jacksonport, is probably the business operation of John Reynolds. Even the "cedar king," Joseph Smith of Jacksonport, whose lumber business reached annual revenues of $130,000, left the lumber business and began farming.

Demand for lumber products became especially heavy after the Civil War. Railroad ties, fence posts, and telegraph poles were in great demand throughout the nation. The Chicago and Peshtigo Fires in 1871 also contributed to the demand. Power tools in the 1880s made possible the large scale production of lumber products. On Washington Island, during this period, large loads could be pulled over the ice and snow by one-horse-drawn sleds. (Courtesy of Washington Island Archives.)

During the late 1860s an area just south of Baileys Harbor was a busy commercial center with a sawmill, hotel, and other commercial ventures all prospering. As the amount of wood available began to dwindle, those who remained turned to farming. A load of some 800 cords of wood were stored on a long pier waiting for shipment when a storm collapsed the pier. Many farmers were forced to abandon the area. Never able to recover the expected payment for their logs, they could not pay their mortgages. The area was used by campers in the early decades of the 20th century.

Ships of all sizes carried the many types of logs transported through Sturgeon Bay. (Courtesy of Door County Maritime Museum.)

A schooner hauls a load of lumber and what appear to be cedar posts through the Sturgeon Bay Canal around 1900. (Courtesy of Joanne M. Mathes and Door County Maritime Museum.)

The sawmill came to Jacksonport around 1900. The equipment was the property of Christ Spille (on left near driver's seat), who, as a farmer, also owned the threshing machine and the sawmill. (Courtesy of James Halstead Sr. and the Jacksonport Historical Society.)

The Louis Prueter Mill Company, a sawmill in Baileys Harbor, is pictured here in the early 20th century. A few years after this photo was taken, reflecting the changing status of the economy from forestry to farming, the mill was converted into a flour mill. (Courtesy of Allen Erickson.)

The sawmill at Rowleys Bay, seen here around 1900, stood between the shore and County Highway ZZ. It measured about 60 feet by 30 feet and was about 25 feet tall. The current owner of the property has written, "Sawing logs created immense piles of sawdust. Some of the remains were left to rot and make fill where some cottages now stand." Some of the sawdust was used to cover and preserve ice until the summer. This method of "refrigeration" was used until the 1950s in Rowleys Bay. (Courtesy of Leonard Peterson.)

Christian Saabye was the only known Finn to settle on Washington Island. Around 1915 he built a gristmill near Washington Harbor that was later used as a lumber mill. The operations lasted about ten years. (Courtesy of Washington Island Archives.)

With a sailboat ready to leave with a shipment of wood from Washington Island, Art Hansen may have just borrowed a piece of wood from the shipment to "manufacture" a spar necessary to support the rigging of the sailboat. (Courtesy of Dick Purinton.)

Leland Rogers is hauling a load of wood in Rowleys Bay around 1940. Often youngsters had little opportunity to leave the area where they lived. When Leland visited Shawano for the first time, he wrote about the hard time he had getting used to the cement sidewalks and curbs. It was the first time he ever saw curbs and sidewalks. (Courtesy of Leonard Peterson.)

Albert Carmody stands at the front of his steam engine, which he used to farm his 120 acres in the Carlsville area. The power of the engine is demonstrated as it hauls eight loads of slab wood which was used for firewood and here was probably being taken for transport by boat. (Courtesy of the Door County Museum.)

This is an early island ferry dock, perhaps the one built in 1932, on Washington Island. Since docks faced perilous futures due to storms and heavy winds, there were numerous docks established on Washington Island over the years. The docks in or near Washington Harbor (on the north end of Washington Island) included the wood dock (1873), quarry dock (1873), a second quarry dock (1875), and Foss (Gasoline Town) Dock (1891). Docks near Jackson Harbor on the northeast in Washington Island included the Hansen dock (1885), Christenson dock (1904), McDonald's dock (1904), and Swenson's dock (1915). Freyburg's Mill and dock, located at the West Harbor, were established in 1878. Docks on Detroit Island, at the south end of Detroit Harbor, included the Hill's Fish dock (1883), Hill Boat Line dock (1891), and Jorgenson dock (1896). Most docks on Washington Island were built in Detroit Harbor. On the west side of the harbor were the Erickson dock (1895), Cornell dock (1907), Chambers dock (1910), and the Shellswick dock (1930). Docks on the east side of Detroit Harbor included the Wickman dock (1872), Johnson dock (1875), Koyen dock (1875), Saabye dock (1877), Bowman dock (1879), and the B.L. Anderson dock (1895). The docks and other points of historical interest were drawn for a map issued by the United States Engineer's Office of Milwaukee, Wisconsin, dated November 1, 1939. The map is available at the Washington Island Archives. Other sources identify Ranney's dock as the main dock on Washington Island during the 1850s. (Courtesy of Dick Purinton.)

Foss Dock, or "Gasoline Town," is in Washington Harbor on Washington Island. The Foss Dock and surrounding area were very active around 1900. Fishing was a major occupation since the early 1850s, when fishing became profitable. By the 1860s fishermen were shipping as many as 20,000 barrels of fish from Washington Island in a single season. Whitefish and trout, often weighing 50 to 60 pounds each, filled the barrels. There were numerous fishermen who frequently caught more than a hundred trout a day using a hook and line.

On the right is a mound of fill for the dock crib, as storms frequently washed out the regular fill and the dock was subject to major damage. The term "Gasoline Town" was associated with the dock since it was the first to provide gasoline service to steamers making the voyage around the peninsula. (Courtesy of Washington Island Archives.)

Featured here is a view of the Anderson Dock around 1930. The large building was a warehouse which stored the materials sold at the Anderson store. (Courtesy of Mary Wilson.)

Here is one of the many private cabins on the grounds that later became the Peninsula State Park in 1909, when about two-thirds of the current park was acquired. Many of the cabins were year-round dwellings. Each had a wood-burning fireplace, and many had barrels at the edge of the building to catch rainwater. Even after the park acquired the land, some residents were given lifetime tenancies, and some stayed well into the 1950s. Most who stayed were farmers. The total area of the Peninsula State Park in 1998 was 3,776 acres. (Courtesy of Peninsula State Park Archives.)

The root cellar in Jacksonport can still be seen near Highway 57 in the Erskine Rest Area. It was built during the 1860s and was owned by the Erskine family from 1873 until 1965. The cellar was dug 4 feet deep into the ground. There was a potato bin on one side. In other areas were stone crocks with sourkraut and pickles. Eggs, rutabagas, carrots, and other crops were also preserved. The walls were insulated, and even though the temperatures reached 20 below zero in winter, inside temperatures stayed constant and never reached the freezing point.

In the early 20th century, oats and other grains were cut and bound into shocks on Door County farms. Several shocks were placed together by hand and left to dry. This procedure of harvesting grains was used until the 1930s. (Original photography by W.C. Schroeder; courtesy of Roger Schroeder.)

On County Trunk V near Jacksonport, around 1890, a frame for John Sargent's barn was raised in two days by the farm community with the help of a contractor. It took about two months to finish the barn. Cedar, pine, balsam, or spruce was usually the wood of choice. Tamarack was sometimes used, but it was difficult to drive nails through and more difficult to pull them out. Basements were made from rocks the farmer collected. Mortar made of lime, sand, and water held the stones together. Carpenters did the cutting of timbers and boards. In earlier days big timbers were held together by wooden pegs. The holes for the pegs were drilled out using a 2-inch hand drill. Roofs were usually made from 2-inch by 6-inch timbers, covered by boards and then by wooden shingles. Shingles were often only available in all different widths since knots were cut out before a shingle was made. Once the roof was completed, a concrete floor was laid. (Courtesy of James Halstead Sr. and the Jacksonport Historical Society.)

Potatoes were the agricultural crop on Washington Island for almost 100 years. After William Wickman brought the first Icelanders to Washington Island around 1870, they immediately set up small farms of 2 to 10 acres and began harvesting potatoes. Transporting potatoes to the mainland was not without risk. In 1901 the schooner *Pride* left the island with a load of potatoes. It soon lost its maneuverability and crashed into the rocks. Only 100 bushels of the 900 bushels of potatoes on board could be saved when the *Pride* went aground near Foss Island. The *Pride*'s owner, Chris Klingenberg, sold his island property, moved to Racine, and, in time, paid off each farmer who lost his shipment. Washington Island potato production peaked in the early 1960s at about 200,000 bushels. Poor potato prices and competition from and greater demand for the "processed" potato used for french fries eroded the market for the potatoes grown on Washington Island. (Courtesy of Dick Purinton.)

Six men owned the steam engine that provided threshing service in the mid-peninsula during the 1920s. After completing work on their own farms, the men took the threshing machine to other farmers during the harvest. Posing with their machine are John Seiler, Richard Staver, Eric Mueller, Albert Smith, A.W. Smith, and Oscar Smith. The scene above is believed to be near today's Hardiman Gallery on Highway F. (Courtesy of Eunice Rutherford.)

The Rosewood Factory and General Store, today's Renard's Cheese on Highway S in southern Door County, is pictured here on a typical day around 1895, when farmers would bring their milk to have it processed into cheese. It was estimated that about 5,500 pounds of milk could have been processed "on a real good day" at that time. (Courtesy of Howard Renard.)

It took approximately six hours to make about one vat of cheese at Renard's Cheese on Highway S in southern Door County around 1910. Each worker is holding a "daisy" of cheese, which weighed about 22 pounds. (Courtesy of Howard Renard.)

The cheddar cheese is being examined in the curing room at Renard's Cheese around 1910, in southern Door County on Route S. One hundred pounds of milk and 20 days were needed to make approximately 10 pounds of cheddar cheese. (Courtesy of Howard Renard.)

The Washington Island creamery was destroyed by fire in 1889 and replaced by a cheese factory at the same location. Islanders, reported the *Door County Advocate*, said residents now "shall make their own Limburger." (Courtesy of Dick Purinton.)

Lack of rail service to the Door peninsula after the Civil War, in the view of one historian, was, "in effect, leaving Door County isolated from the rest of the Midwest." While Green Bay had 35 trains moving through it daily, Door County had none. In 1888 there were fears that wood could not be delivered to Sturgeon Bay, and people would not be able to heat their homes. Reluctance to build a railroad stemmed from arguments that the peninsula was well served by the shipping industry, and that a railroad bridge would hinder navigation through Sturgeon Bay. During the 1890s, a bond issue of $600,000 was approved by the County and grants totaling $76,000 were awarded. The Ahnapee (Algoma) and Western Railroad began construction of the railroad that would complete 32 miles of track from Algoma to Sturgeon Bay. The railroad opened August 9, 1894, with the largest crowd ever assembled in Door County in attendance. The turn-around bridge shown above took 20 minutes to open, allow a ship through, close, and realign the rails. (Courtesy of Door County Maritime Museum.)

Sturgeon Bay had a toll bridge between 1887 and 1931. Up to 1914, the maximum rates for crossing were as follows: 75¢ for threshing outfits; 25¢ for team and driver; 15¢ for horse and rider; and 5¢ each for loose sheep, hogs, and foot passengers. Fierce competition between the bridge operators and ferry lines reduced rates during rate wars, such as the one in 1887, which almost abolished many of the rates. The charter to operate the bridge was terminated in 1911, and the City operated the bridge as a utility. After the railroad started using the bridge in 1894, monumental traffic jams began to develop as more and more automobiles used the bridge in the 1920s, and there was pronounced agitation for a second bridge for highway traffic only. (Courtesy of Gloria Hansen.)

The "Last chance to ride the bridge over Sturgeon Bay" was July 3, 1931, when the City of Sturgeon Bay terminated the operation of its toll bridge and turned over the operation of the bridge to the railroad company. The new free bridge, the highway bridge, was opened for traffic a few weeks earlier. (Courtesy of Gloria Hansen.)

By 1867 there was a road between Sturgeon Bay and Baileys Harbor. However, a major, improved road became a necessity. The construction of what became Highway 57 was launched around 1915. It was the first major highway through Door County. Steam-powered engines were used to remove stumps and long roots, such as that in the center of the photo above. (Courtesy of James Halstead Sr. and the Jacksonport Historical Society.)

The Sturgeon Bay Stone Company was located about 3 miles north of Sturgeon Bay. The above photo was taken when the quarry was in full operation during the 1920s. After business fell off in the 1930s, the quarry was razed and then moved to Drummond Island, the eastern-most island in Michigan's Upper Peninsula. The dismantling was done by C. Ray Christianson of Sturgeon Bay and it was loaded on barges for the trip to Drummond Island. The quarry was abandoned by 1950. Cement foundations can still be found at the old site.

Quarries in the Sturgeon Bay area included the Sturgeon Bay Stone Company (west); Queen Quarry, Brewster Quarry, located west of Sturgeon Bay, and the Leathem and Smith Quarry; Sturgeon Bay Stone Company (east); and Lauries Quarry, located east of Sturgeon Bay.

Numerous buildings in Door County were constructed using the limestone from quarries in the Sturgeon Bay area, including the St. Joseph Church in Sturgeon Bay, St. John the Baptist Church in Egg Harbor, the Bank of Sturgeon Bay (now the Harmann Studios), and the former Sturgeon Bay Library, which is currently used as an office building. (Original photography by W.C. Schroeder; courtesy of Roger Schroeder.)

The Leathem and Smith Quarry was located at the north end of Sturgeon Bay. The above photo was taken in 1977, but the appearance of the quarry had not changed since the early 1930s, when the quarry was abandoned. The quarry was fully operational during the 1870s, trying to meet the great demands for limestone necessary to rebuild after the Chicago and Peshtigo fires of 1871. At the time, workers were making about $1 per day. Various commercial ventures were proposed for the site. Since there were concerns about how the ecology of the area would be affected by such plans, the State of Wisconsin purchased the property and still owns it today. (Courtesy of Bill Skadden.)

Since the steam-powered engine was horse drawn, the above view is probably the Leathem and Smith Quarry north of Sturgeon Bay, where ships, because of the depth of the water, could pull up close to the shoreline for loading. The quarries in the Little Sturgeon Bay area required long piers since the water was very shallow and ships could not come close to the shoreline. (Courtesy of Door County Maritime Museum.)

Pictured here is a crusher building at a quarry, probably in the Sturgeon Bay area. Stone was broken up into small pieces called rip-rap. These pieces were small enough to use around the shore area and could be easily moved. Much of the rip-rap was put into lime kilns, which were timber fired. After the water was driven, or cooked out of the limestone, it became quick lime, which had many commercial, industrial, agricultural, and domestic uses. Most buildings throughout Door County in the late 19th century and early 20th century were white, probably painted with a quick-lime solution. Although it did not last very long, quick lime was plentiful and very affordable. (Courtesy of Door County Maritime Museum.)

At the quarries, overhead conveyer belts were constructed to take the limestone from the crushing building to storage bins. The above photo was taken around 1910. (Courtesy of Door County Maritime Museum.)

As the sizes of the quarries grew larger and stone was being mined farther away from the shoreline, it was necessary to build rail lines and use steam-powered engines to move stone for loading before shipment. It is believed the above photo was taken during the 1920s. (Courtesy of Fritz Brunswilk.)

Steam-powered shovels would scoop up limestone after dynamite blasting. The shovels, in the words of a scholar who has studied the operation of the quarries of Door County, "were enormously powerful." They could pick up 5 to 10 yards in one scoop of stone weighing as much as 20 tons. (Courtesy of Door County Maritime Museum.)

Stone is being loaded onto a barge at one of the quarries north of Sturgeon Bay around 1900. Barges of this type were used for the larger pieces of stone that often measured as much as 6 feet in diameter and weighed around 10 tons each. Stone of this size and weight were particularly useful at harbor entrances and to build piers. Waves, rising to 25 feet during heavy storms, would often wash away smaller piers fortified with only smaller rocks. (Courtesy of Door County Maritime Museum.)

During the first decade of the 20th century, Sturgeon Bay enjoyed a building boom. Traditionally only wooden structures were built throughout the city. However, with the population having doubled and numerous commercial businesses thriving, the city, which had a plentiful supply of stone within a few miles, began building commercial, residential, and city buildings out of stone. Employment was plentiful, including work for 100 stonemasons, who were busy throughout the year building such structures as the Sturgeon Bay City Hall. (Courtesy of Eldred Koepsel.)

Fishing for herring was popular near Fish Creek in the early 1900s. About 80 percent of the population in the Fish Creek area depended on fishing for their livelihood at the turn of the century. At that time, no licenses were necessary to fish, and a good catch, such as the one above, could haul in about 600 pounds in a lift. Another source of income for residents was servicing the many boats that stopped at Fish Creek for refueling. (Courtesy of Gibraltar Historical Association.)

Ice harvesting started as a major business in the Sturgeon Bay area around 1870, when Albert Marshall Spear built a 50,000-ton ice-block storage house, which he later sold to the Piper Ice Company. Piper, who added five more warehouses, employed 100 men to cut and store the ice from Little Sturgeon Bay. Sawdust—there was plenty due to the sawmills—was spread on the ice to keep it from melting. Eventually, every village had its own ice business. Much of the ice remained available for shipping until the summer, when it was shipped to markets as distant as Chicago. (Courtesy of the Door County Museum.)

The *Wisconsin* began auto ferry service in 1923 between Gills Rock and Washington Island. The *Wisconsin* held four cars, one big and three small. The cars were loaded with the use of planks and then lashed to the rail. Previously the boat had been used for hauling freight from Green Bay, Escanaba, Garden, and Nahma (in the Upper Peninsula of Michigan). The *Wisconsin* was used for ferry service until 1929, when it was replaced by the *Welcome*, which could carry ten cars. (Courtesy of Dick Purinton.)

The *Welcome* ferry arrives at Rowleys Bay on Lake Michigan with a truck load of fresh fish caught around Washington Island. The ferry dock had been in use in Rowleys Bay since 1931. It was used only when the weather did not permit a safe landing at Gills Rock on Green Bay. Numerous complications arose since neither crew nor passengers would know weather conditions, particularly wind currents, in "Death's Door," after leaving Washington Island. When the wind was from the northwest, the ferry would likely dock at Rowleys Bay. Often passengers and crew believed they were going to Gills Rock until they experienced the wind a mile or two out of Detroit Harbor on Washington Island. (Courtesy of Leonard Peterson.)

Children of all ages in Door County, and others from surrounding areas and as far away as Mexico, were brought in for the cherry-picking harvest in Door County. Many children from other areas, who worked in the cherry orchards of Door County, attended school in Door County and were able to retain and practice their cultural and religious observances. For example, children from Mexico were prepared to receive their first Holy Communion at St. Peter and Paul Church in Institute, north of Sturgeon Bay.

Cherries were picked in buckets (left) and then sorted on large tables to eliminate those which were damaged or unfit for packaging in large crates. Competition to determine the fastest pickers often developed. Around 1928, a record 1,020 quarts was set at the Martin Orchard in 15 hours and 30 minutes. After that record was announced, several pickers claimed they were collecting as many as 1,400 quarts in 13.5-hour days. The record that went unmatched was made in 1929, when a 17 year old picked 1,419 quarts in 13 hours and 10 minutes. (Courtesy of Eva Kita.)

The population of Door County swelled by the thousands as workers streamed into the area for cherry picking. During the 1940s and 1950s, Native Americans from several reservations in Wisconsin were brought to the Proctor Orchards near Egg Harbor. The Native Americans lived in tents and had their own cook house. Most remained for the entire picking season, which usually lasted for six weeks, from the Fourth of July until the end of August. (Courtesy of Eva Kita.)

German prisoners of war began working in Door County's cherry orchards around 1944. Many had light-colored fatigue caps, and some observers speculated that they were probably members of the Afrika Corps. Although the prisoner, clearly marked as a "POW," appears to be closely guarded by a single soldier with a rifle, most prisoners were not so closely guarded, and some worked in the orchards without guards. (Original photography by W.C. Schroeder; courtesy of Roger Schroeder.)

Cherry-picking season attracted all types of participants, including young ladies in long dresses. Shown above are Inga Bavry Mueller, Emily Bavry Anderson, and Ethel Bavry Enigl. The above photo was taken around 1920. These types of scenes were probably commonplace in the following years and perhaps helped formulate the idea of selecting a cherry blossom queen. In 1929 a queen was selected, and Sturgeon Bay celebrated with a parade and three-day historical pageant. (Courtesy of John Enigl.)

The Cherry Blossom Queen poses in this photo, probably around 1930, with a load of cherries about to leave Door County during the Cherry Harvest Festival. The railroad which served Door County was the Anapee and Western, a division of the Green Bay and Western Railroad. (Original photography by W.C. Schroeder; courtesy of Roger Schroeder.)

This is an aerial view of the Fruit Growers Cooperative in the late 1930s. Thousands of containers filled with brine for the production of maraschino cherries are loaded on the docks awaiting shipment. On the right are the Peterson Boat Works.

To try to envision the major impact cherries had on the economy of Door County at this time, it must be known that between 12,000 and 15,000 workers were "imported" to pick the crop. In 1923, grades were established to determine quality. An estimated 35,000 trees were planted in 1923, even though 400,000 were already under cultivation in 1923. By 1927 another 50,000 trees were added. The following year some 500 acres of new trees (at 100 per acre) were added. By the end of the 1920s, Door County farmers were thinking of expanding cherry operations to Michigan. However, the Great Depression and hardships of the 1930s kept such ideas from being implemented. (Original photography by W.C. Schroeder; courtesy of Roger Schroeder.)

Fresh cherries were usually packed in crates which were loaded on wagons and taken to Sturgeon Bay for shipment. In 1922, perhaps the year the above photo was taken, some 88,725 pounds of fresh cherries were shipped in a single day by parcel post and express from the mail terminal in Sturgeon Bay.

Numerous promotions were employed to encourage the use of cherries grown in Door County. Thousands of reprints of favorite recipes using cherries were distributed without charge through hundreds of outlets. (Courtesy of Eva Kita.)

A shipment of Door County cherries cross the old Sturgeon Bay Railroad bridge, which was just north of the present-day downtown bridge. The railroad cars let everyone know this is "A whole train load of cherries [being] shipped to markets of the world." This promotion of Door County cherries to the growers and the Fruit Growers Canning Company incurred only the cost of the paintings on the railroad cars. (Original photography by W.C. Schroeder; courtesy of Roger Schroeder.)

The workers at the Fruit Growers Cooperative appear to be enjoying a break during the cherry harvest season, probably in the late 1930s. (Original photography by W.C. Schroeder; courtesy of Roger Schroeder.)

The passage to Washington Island from the northern Door peninsula was usually frozen throughout the winter. This photo of that area was taken around 1900. The only possible way to get the mail to the island was over the frozen water passage. Beginning in the 1890s, Nels Jepson made an effort twice a month to get the mail to Washington Island. The above photo was taken in the vicinity of Plum Island. (Courtesy of Dick Purinton.)

During the early years of postal service in Door County, managing the post office in the local community was often considered a status symbol. The owner of the general store, usually the high-traffic area in the community, was frequently the postmaster. Often, Door County post offices were named for individuals. The Leccia post office (near Brussels) was named in honor of Rev. Erasmus Leccia, who established an Independent Catholic Society, which rejected Papal authority. Located next to St. Michael's Church, it lasted from 1880 to 1885. The Marcus post office was named for Marcus McCormick, the first postmaster of the village that later became Forestville. The Fagerwick ("beautiful bay" in Danish) post office was in operation on Washington Island from 1881 through 1882. The above residence of the postmaster in Detroit Harbor on Washington Island is that of Bo Anderson, who was the first to hold this post, serving from 1892 to 1907. The date of the photo is 1904.

The Sister Bay, Wisconsin Post Office, which opened in 1873, is pictured here around 1915. It was converted into a grocery store, owned by Mary Bunda and, afterwards, by her son, William. The building eventually burned down. (Courtesy of Allen Erickson.)

The Jacksonport post office was in service from 1867 to 1970, when the office was closed. Postal service officially came to Door County June 22, 1854, when the first regular post office opened at Washington Harbor on the north end of Washington Island. As roads cut through the interior of the peninsula, more post offices were established. By the end of 1862, 12 post offices were in operation. By 1880, there were 24 post offices throughout the county. At one time or another there were 48 named post offices in Door County. By 1910 only 13 post offices remained. In 1998 Door County was served by 11 post offices: Baileys Harbor, Brussels, Egg Harbor, Ellison Bay, Ephraim, Fish Creek, Forestville, Maplewood, Sister Bay, Sturgeon Bay, and Washington Island.

The Erskine family of Jacksonport often made maple syrup. The family is pictured here around 1910. They owned a large tract of land on which they gathered sap and cooked it into syrup. Other families collected sap as a means of supplementing the family income. During the 1920s, a gallon of maple syrup brought $5. Some families could collect enough sap to make and sell as many as 100 gallons a year.

In this early-20th-century photograph, maple sap is being boiled down into syrup. Sap pails held about 5 gallons each. A person could collect and fill three barrels in a morning when the sap was flowing the best, which was on a warm spring day after a cold freezing night. Sap is still gathered throughout Door County and processed and sold as maple syrup. (Original photography by W.C. Schroeder; courtesy of Roger Schroeder.)

Scofield Company hardware store is pictured here in 1881 in Sturgeon Bay. The store is the current site of the Pudgy Seagull restaurant. Scofield moved his store in 1903 and remained in business at that site until 1953, when that property on Third Street was sold at auction. (Courtesy of Bill and Fran Cecil.)

Wilson Ice Cream Parlor opened in Ephraim in 1906 and continues in operation to the present day. It was a summer business which made its own ice cream—for sale at the parlor and for delivery by boat to the people who lived close to the shore. Oscar Wilson, the owner, was a former candy worker in Milwaukee. He made his own chocolate and caramel sauces, which he blended into ice cream that was sold for 5¢ a scoop. (Courtesy of Mary Wilson.)

Leonard Pfeifer and his son, Alex, are ready to cut the meat in Leonard Proctor's Butcher Shop at 60 West Maple in West Sturgeon Bay around 1900. In later years the shop was known as the John Haen Market. (Courtesy of the Door County Museum.)

This is the interior of the Charles Greison store in downtown Sturgeon Bay around 1916. Shown in the photo are Mary Simon De Schmid, Nora Fidler, Clifford Greisen, Mrs. Charles Greisen, and Charles Greisen. The name "Greison" can still be seen at the top of the building at 164 North Third Street in Sturgeon Bay. (Courtesy of the Door County Museum.)

The Bay View House in Sawyer (Sturgeon Bay) provided lodging for travelers and workers. Philopina, wife of owner John Goettleman, always wanted her own house, so John had the kitchen of the Bay View House sawed off (extreme left) and moved away from the building. Philopina had her "own" house. The Bay View House was located in today's area of Madison and Oak Streets. In this 1900 photo, a shipment of beer from the Sturgeon Bay Brewery arrived. The brewery was established by Louis and Ernest Leidiger during the 1870s. It was reported that "Theirs was a quality beer and they found ready buyers for all they could brew." The Sturgeon Bay Brewery was bought out by Hagemeister, a Green Bay brewing company, which operated the Sturgeon Bay plant as a branch. (Courtesy of Goettelman family collections.)

Pictured here are the Pinney Building, post office annex, and Wisconsin Telephone Company building in Sturgeon Bay around 1912. It was written that "the most striking building of the period was the Pinney Building, completed in 1906. The three-story structure was built at the corner of Cedar (Third) and Michigan. It was, without a doubt, the most imposing building of the city." (Courtesy of Allen Erickson.)

Hans Hansen had a taxi business that serviced Washington Island and the mainland of northern Door County. In winter, the taxi had to cross on ice. With his big Buick, Hansen was taking a lady to the hospital in 1923. Although he had a track, he ventured farther west and did not calculate that a southwest wind might affect the thickness of the ice. When he got on ice that was 4.5 inches thick, the back wheel went through the ice. The Coast Guard from Plum Island pried the back end of the car but accidentally punctured a hole in the gas tank. No reports are available about whether or when the woman got to the hospital. (Courtesy of Dick Purinton.)

The People's Hospital was one of several hospitals in the Sturgeon Bay area in the early 1900s. Others were the Whitelaw Sanitarium, Physicians Hospital, Hilton Hospital, Egeland Hospital, and P and S Hospital. Some consisted of only one room. Before 1923 patients with broken bones had to be X-rayed in Green Bay. In 1923 Dr. G.E. Egeland began using an X-ray machine in Sturgeon Bay. Sturgeon Bay physicians made house calls as far away as Egg Harbor, Brussels, and Jacksonport. (Courtesy of Henry A. Anderson, M.D.)

The Felhofer Brothers built a blacksmith shop in and around Valmy, a few miles north of Sturgeon Bay, in 1912. Business was very good, and a Ford garage was built. After Ed Felhofer returned from World War I, he studied engineering, and a new garage was built in 1922. A garage still services autos on the same site in today's Valmy. (Original photography by W.C. Schroeder; courtesy of Roger Schroeder.)

The Cities Service gas station opened in downtown Jacksonport between 1933 and 1934. It was owned by Fred Erskine and Henry Spille. Gasoline was about 10¢ a gallon when it opened and almost doubled in price by the late 1930s, when many people in the area had their own automobiles. (Courtesy of James Halstead Sr. and the Jacksonport Historical Association.)

Three

SHIPS AND SHIPBUILDING

The *Marion* was specifically designed for Herbert C. Scofield, one of the early mayors of Sturgeon Bay. It is said to be the first boat built by Peterson Boat Works around 1915. Martin Peterson built a small shop behind his personal residence at 505 South Cedar Street (now Memorial Drive) over the water to work on this boat. The boat was used as a pleasure craft. Scofield co-owned a shipbuilding company, which he sold to Fred Peterson's father, which then became the Peterson Boat Works. (Courtesy of Bill and Fran Cecil.)

This view of Sturgeon Bay Canal looking east toward Lake Michigan was probably taken around 1890. Joseph Harris Sr. was a strong believer in the necessity of the building of this canal, which would connect Sturgeon Bay with Lake Michigan and save 100 miles for anyone wanting to make the trip from the city of Green Bay to Chicago or to other points east of the bay of Green Bay. Harris began his efforts to have a canal built around 1860. However, it was not until March 5, 1868, when the Wisconsin State Legislature made possible the building of the canal. There were further delays for four years, and the first shovel of dirt for the canal was scooped July 8, 1872. Shortages of funds prevented rapid completion of the canal until June 28, 1878, when the waters of Sturgeon Bay and Lake Michigan co-mingled for the first time. An opening was made and allowed "Captain" W.T. Casgain, engineer of the canal, to cross this passageway in a rowboat. The canal, 7,400 feet long and 100 feet wide, cost $291,461.69 in 1881 when it was inspected by government officials and declared completed. (Courtesy of Joanne M. Mathes and Door County Maritime Museum.)

Pictured here is the tugboat *George Nelson* and her tow of five schooners filled with lumber. They were heading east through the Sturgeon Bay Canal in 1892, bound for the Chicago market. The *Nelson* was owned by Leathem and Smith of Sturgeon Bay. (Courtesy of Joanne M. Mathes and Door County Maritime Museum.)

A steam tug pulls a load through Sturgeon Bay Canal, probably around 1900. (Courtesy of Joanne M. Mathes and Door County Maritime Museum.)

This postal card, dated 1909, shows the Sturgeon Bay Canal station and probably one of the Goodrich Boats that frequently toured in the area. (Courtesy of Allen Erickson.)

The *Ann Arbor Number Five* was built in Toledo and launched in 1910. When used as an ice breaker (seen here), she was making her way from Sturgeon Bay to Menominee through Green Bay in mid-winter. Normally *Ann Arbor Number Five* broke ice when it was 2 feet thick. However, she was known to go through ice 36 inches thick and once pushed her way through 20 feet of water where the ice extended to the bottom. During her day, *Ann Arbor Number Five* was also known as the fastest boat to clear a pathway through the ice of Green Bay. (Courtesy of Door County Maritime Museum.)

The Ann Arbor Railroad provided railroad car ferry service in the Sturgeon Bay area. The *Ann Arbor Car Ferry Number Three* made the trip through the Sturgeon Bay Canal around 1900. The maiden voyage of the *Ann Arbor Number Three* was November 11, 1898. It was 258 feet long, with the beam at 58 feet across. Besides railroad cars, the ship also transported grain and other forms of freight. (Courtesy of Door County Maritime Museum.)

This photo of Smith Shipbuilding in Sturgeon Bay shows small freighters under construction for Great Britain during World War II. These freighters were probably under construction in 1943, which was considered the peak of the war effort when a ship a week was being produced for the United States Navy. (Original photography by W.C. Schroeder; courtesy of Roger Schroeder.)

Here is a view inside the plate shop at Smith Shipbuilding of Sturgeon Bay. Sections of the ship were built inside the plate shop. One section could weigh as much as 100 tons and stand as high as 30 feet. The sections would be moved by a gantry, a heavy lift crane, to the ship for assembly. (Original photography by W.C. Schroeder; courtesy of Roger Schroeder.)

This aerial view of Smith Shipbuilding in Sturgeon Bay was taken during World War II. Identifiable in the photo are sub-chasers and corvettes under construction. The photo had a large circulation since it was used as a Christmas greeting card by Smith Shipbuilding. (Original photography by W.C. Schroeder; courtesy of Roger Schroeder.)

Riebolt and Walter Company opened their shipyard in Sturgeon Bay in 1896. When World War I started, 200 were employed at the shipyard. Riebolt and Walter became Universal Shipbuilding in 1918, and then, in 1926, Sturgeon Bay Ship Building and Dry Dock Company. The company prospered during World War II, and the areas surrounding the shipyard were called "boomtowns." (Original photo by Herb Reynolds; courtesy of Mary Reynolds Aiken and Door County Maritime Museum.)

After working for the Sturgeon Bay Boat Manufacturing Company for two years until it closed in 1907, Martin Peterson acquired some waterfront property in Sturgeon Bay and opened his Peterson Boat Works in 1908. Economic hardships associated with World War I caused him to delay the operation of his own company, and he worked for the Leathem and Smith Dock Company. He reopened Peterson Boat Works in 1933. His business doubled every year during the 1930s, and he built vessels for the United States Army Corps of Engineers during World War II. When the war ended, Peterson Boat Works changed its name to Peterson Builders. (Courtesy of Door County Maritime Museum.)

The Peterson Boat Works is pictured here around 1942. Wood patrol crafts were being constructed for the United States Navy. Peterson received its first order from the United States Navy to build personnel boats in 1939. They also built 110-foot sub-chasers, mine sweepers, wooden rescue boats, and other vessels for the war effort. (Original photography by W.C. Schroeder; courtesy of Roger Schroeder.)

Ships' propellers were guarded by the United States Coast Guard during the 1942–1945 period, when hundreds of ships were built in Sturgeon Bay for the United States Navy. Shipyards were working seven days a week, three shifts a day. (Original photography by W.C. Schroeder; courtesy of Roger Schroeder.)

Women shipyard workers in Sturgeon Bay were a common sight during World War II. The ladies above appear to be wedging up a ship hull for launching. At the peak of the war effort, some 750 women were employed in the shipyards. (Original photography by W.C. Schroeder; courtesy of Roger Schroeder.)

In response to Sturgeon Bay's booming shipbuilding industry during World War II, two major housing developments, Sunrise and Sunset, were provided for workers. Sunrise, shown above, had connected units built in block formation. These were constructed from prefabricated sections and were two-story multiple dwellings. Sunset consisted of detached individual units. Although some claimed the buildings did not wear well and came down as fast as they went up, several were still in use in 1998. The Dun-Ro-Min and Shorewood Motels utilize several units today. Other units are on the Nebel property at Fifteenth and Rhode Island and near the junction of Highways 42 and 57 north of Sturgeon Bay. (Courtesy of the Door County Museum.)

The *Clement T. Jayne* was launched April 30, 1943, from the Leathem D. Smith shipyard in Sturgeon Bay. It was one of ten coastal cargo ships built by the shipyard. After World War II began, there was a dramatic rise in shipbuilding in Sturgeon Bay. In 1940 there were 300 men working at the Leathem shipyard. Within six months, 1,500 were employed. By the end of the war, some 5,600 were employed at Sturgeon Bay's shipyards. Contracts came so rapidly that docks had to be built at the same time that ships were being constructed on those same docks. (Courtesy of Leonard Peterson.)

A view of Whitefish Bay on April 4, 1949, indicates how marine traffic was affected when the steamer Benson Ford was grounded in the channel at Sturgeon Bay. Southbound traffic had to be anchored until the Benson Ford was set afloat. (Courtesy of Door County Maritime Museum.)

The *Marjelea* was built by the Sturgeon Bay Shipbuilding and Dry Dock Company in Sturgeon Bay in 1947. The *Marjelea* was used as a tow boat, or push boat, on the Mississippi River. (Original photo by Herb Reynolds; courtesy of Mary Reynolds Aiken and Door County Maritime Museum.)

The *Fountain City* was built in 1857, with a length of 210 feet and a 31-foot beam. The *Fountain City* caught fire just before midnight on May 5, 1896, and her lines burned. She drifted away from the dock onto a mud bank. Although the fire department was able to extinguish the flames, the ship was declared a total loss by her owners in the morning. Most of her machinery was destroyed and her wooden hull was declared worthless. The above photo shows her stern under water in Sturgeon Bay. The photo was taken by Bert Scofield and developed in his own darkroom, which he had at his residence. Remains of the boat are still in Sturgeon Bay to the present day. (Courtesy of Bill and Fran Cecil.)

Pictured here are the remains of a wrecked ship in the Sturgeon Bay Canal around 1900. (Courtesy of Joanne M. Mathes and Door County Maritime Museum.)

WRECK PRIDE, ICED DOWN IN WASHINGTON HARBOR, WIS.

In 1901 the schooner *Pride* left Washington Harbor on Washington Island with a load of potatoes. It soon lost its maneuverability and grounded on the rocks near the Foss dock. Only 100 of the 900 bushels of potatoes on board could be saved when the *Pride* went aground near Foss Island. The *Pride*'s owner, Chris Klingenberg, sold his island property, moved to Racine, and, in time, paid off each farmer who lost his shipment. (Courtesy of Dick Purinton.)

The Eagle Bluff Lighthouse in Peninsula State Park near Fish Creek was built in 1868. The above photo, taken around 1900, also shows the oil house, or fuel house, in the center and a building on the right which is no longer there. The second keeper of the lighthouse, William Duclon, won several citations for having "the best looking lighthouse grounds in the Great Lakes area." Duclon and his wife had eight sons. Duclon remained the lighthouse keeper for 35 years until 1918. He and Mrs. Duclon are buried in Blossomburg Cemetery in the Peninsula State Park. (Courtesy of Peninsula State Park Archives.)

The Cana Island Lighthouse was built of yellow brick in 1869. It is 89 feet high and located on a small island in Lake Michigan. The island was connected to the mainland by a foot bridge, which became a gravel causeway around 1919. After a storm in 1902, the tower was encased in metal and painted white. An automatic light has been functioning there since the 1940s. (Courtesy of Leonard Peterson.)

The Plum Island Light began operation in 1898 as one of a pair of range lights overlooking Death's Door Passage near Washington Island. The gentleman on the left, dressed in tuxedo with bow tie, poses with a string of freshly caught fish—probably caught by someone else. It was common for a young lad to catch some fish and offer visitors the "catch" for purposes of posing for a photo. The gentleman with the tuxedo and his catch were later featured on a postal card from Plum Island. The gentleman on the right, the light tower, the dock, and the sailboat were all eliminated on the card. (Courtesy of Dick Purinton.)

The Plum Island life-saving crew was stationed on the Door side of Plum Island. The idea of establishing a life-saving station in the area of Washington Island was proposed in late 1891. A dramatic rescue by the Plum Island life-saving crew was reported by the *Door County Advocate* on December 8, 1900. "On arriving (at the stranded) 'Bielman,' (they) found it awash, the heavy seas having washed the cabin in which the crew slept overboard. It is needless to state the arrival of the lifesavers was hailed with delight and the thoroughly alarmed men lost no time in transferring their positions to one in the lifeboat. As there were seventeen on board and the life-boat held seven men, it was found necessary to throw overboard all the ballast in the sailboat to accommodate them. They were . . . successfully transferred . . . in the darkness and sea, and taken back to Plum Island, where they arrived about 7 o'clock and spent the day following in comfort and safety, feeling sure the abandoned steamer would pound to pieces in another 24 hours." (Courtesy of Dick Purinton.)

Four

RELIGION

The Moravian Church in Ephraim is pictured here on the hillside, after a part of it had been moved from the shore. The church was built in 1857, dedicated in 1859, and has seen continuous use to the present day. (Courtesy of Mary Wilson.)

A 4-acre parcel of land was purchased for the Sturgeon Bay congregation of St. Joseph Parish in 1865 for $66, and a church was constructed in 1866. A second church was erected in 1889. A third church, at the time the largest in Sturgeon Bay with a seating capacity of 600, was begun in 1908. The cornerstone was laid May 2, 1910. The dedication (above photo) was November 14, 1910. (Courtesy of St. Joseph Parish Archives.)

The Bethel Church was established on Washington Island in 1865. The Bethel Society was founded in England in 1814 to establish Bethel Seaman Society Chapels in major world ports. By 1831 the American Bethel Society had spread to the Great Lakes area and was providing non-denominational services for seamen. D. Elbert Raney deeded land to the people of Washington Island for a cemetery and a church. The Bethel Society provided financial aid to build the church and subsidized salaries of guest preachers for a few years. The church provided non-denominational services for seamen until 1949 and was also used for community gatherings. The church is still in operation today as an independent Bethel Evangelical Church, welcoming all who work on or visit Washington Island.

Early Sunday-morning worshippers are on the way to Swedish Baptist Church in Sister Bay around 1900. The congregation's first church was built in 1882 on an acre of land donated by H.J. Wiltse on Maple Drive. Stables were added in 1883. The church was later renamed the First Baptist Church of Sister Bay. (Courtesy of First Baptist Church of Sister Bay Archives.)

The Methodist Church of Sturgeon Bay established a congregation in 1863 and a regular pastor, Rev. B.M. Fuller, was assigned. A church was built and dedicated in 1868. The church had a tower 100 feet high that was later cut down and used as a feed store. A second church, above, was built in 1899 and dedicated on October 22. The congregation numbered close to 200 and had about 500 adherents.

Members of the congregation that became the Methodist Church of Sawyer began meeting during the 1860s in a small schoolhouse. A church was built and dedicated in 1868. In April 1911, the church burned to the ground and was replaced by a new stone church dedicated on November 5, 1911. In 1917, Rev. Robert Wilkowski, "the flying preacher," arrived. He was successful in changing the services from German to English, which many preachers of the congregation were not able to do with complete success. (Courtesy of Allen Erickson.)

During the 1870s the Catholic congregation at Egg Harbor, known as St. John of the Desert, became attached to St. Joseph Church in Sturgeon Bay as a regular mission. In 1878 Father Engelbert Blume directed the building of the first church in Egg Harbor. A small log building served the congregation until 1888, when a second church, 30 feet by 40 feet, was built. On December 6, 1908, 17 people met to incorporate as the Congregation of St. John the Baptist Church in Egg Harbor. Land was deeded for the new church by Charles and Delia LaRouche. The dedication on the site where the church still stands was October 5, 1910. (Courtesy of Eva Kita.)

The St. Michael's Catholic Church was built in 1882, after a congregation of 25 families each pledged from $2 to $25 for the $500 needed to build the church. St. Michael's was fortunate to receive artifacts from other churches as they built new facilities. The pews came from a church in Egg Harbor, and the statue of Mary was once in a church in Fish Creek. (Courtesy of James Halstead Sr. and the Jacksonport Historical Society.)

The German Lutheran Church, today's Immanuel Lutheran Church of Baileys Harbor, was built in 1892, after Carl Piel Sr. called a meeting on May 1, 1892, for a congregation of 15 families. Donations for a church site and cemetery were made by Mrs. John Oldenburg and Mrs. Wahltman in May, and building operations began in June 1892. (Courtesy of Immanuel Lutheran Church Archives.)

In 1931 the Immanuel Lutheran Church, built in 1914, was moved from the hilltop on which it stood to street level. A heavy-timbered structure was built and the church was moved eastward to the new site, then lowered downward onto the newly constructed foundation. A squared-off bluff of limestone was used as part of the west wall of the basement. This church was demolished in 1981, and the congregation then worshipped in the church which has served the community to the present day. (Courtesy Immanuel Lutheran Church Archives.)

The Jacksonport Methodist Church was built on land donated by Joseph and Maggie Smith. Construction began in 1890. By July 1891, the foundation was completed. Most of the lumber, material, and labor was furnished by the members of the church. Harry Wilson Sr. and George Bagnall Sr., two members of the church, worked on the structure for several months. The church was completed by early 1893. In the early 1960s, when the church was being redecorated, the parishioners were happy to hear that the building was constructed and had remained perfectly true throughout the years. The church was built without electricity, running water, or indoor plumbing, and remains so until the present day. (Courtesy of James Halstead Sr. and the Jacksonport Historical Association.)

The interior of the Jacksonport Methodist Church, as stated in the centennial history of the church in 1890, "conveys the feeling of simplicity that has continued over the past 100 years." The pews remain straight and were uncushioned until 1994, the altar rail and pulpit are white, and the original Epworth reed organ is still in use. An oil stove replaced a wood-burning stove in the 1940s, and the two ornate chancel chairs were donated in 1949. (Courtesy of James Halstead Sr. and the Jacksonport Historical Society.)

Rev. F. Binder, who came to Jacksonport in 1889, was a minister of the United Methodist Church in Jacksonport. Even though the congregation petitioned to retain the popular Reverend Binder, he chose to leave and preached his last sermon on October 4, 1890. (Courtesy of James Halstead Sr. and the Jacksonport Historical Society.)

The present St. Mary of the Lake Church in Baileys Harbor was built as a result of a bequest of Michael W. McArdle, a native of Baileys Harbor who became a successful businessman. McArdle wrote the following to the congregation: "To the Catholics of Baileys Harbor—Fifty years ago I served on this spot as an altar boy. More than once I tumbled over in a faint from the bitter cold, for I was of delicate constitution—Even then I had an ambition to see a nice comfortable Catholic church here but didn't dream I could ever take part in it. But, I am glad to say all is now ready to go ahead." McArdle passed away in 1935, and the new church was dedicated in 1936. (Courtesy of Eva Kita.)

The first St. Mary of the Snows Church was built in 1860 in Namur. It was a log-cabin structure measuring 30 feet by 40 feet. In 1875 a new church was built to accommodate 100 families. A rectory was added in 1884, and a classroom was constructed in 1889. The church burned down in 1891. A new church and school were built, but they were destroyed by fire the following year during the spring. The photo shows the current St. Mary of the Snows shortly after it was built in 1892, when Highway 57 was still a dirt road. (Courtesy of Harry Chaudoir Sr.)

This is an interior view of the current St. Mary of the Snows Church a few years after it was built (by the summer 1892). Since that time the church has undergone several changes, including replacement of the gas lamps (right, center) with electric lighting. (Courtesy of Harry Chaudoir Sr.)

The Lutheran church in Baileys Harbor (today's Immanuel Lutheran Church) was probably decorated by members of the congregation as they walked into the church during the Christmas season in the 1890s. Each left a toy or trinket on the tree or altar. Most were reminders of their homeland and included models of ships, homes, churches, animals, and traditional German decorations. It is likely that the unidentifiable centerpiece (the rounded column with a lamp on each side) was brought in by a member of the congregation. The current pastor at the church explained that he could not associate the item with anything that may have been used in Lutheran services at any time in the Baileys Harbor area. (Courtesy of Immanuel Lutheran Church Archives.)

This was Harvest celebration at the Hope Congregational Church, later known as the Hope United Church of Christ, in Sturgeon Bay in 1892. The church was founded in 1881. The elaborate display of harvested produce, the dress of the participants, and the wall displays suggest the celebration may have lasted longer than one day. (Courtesy of the Hope United Church of Christ Archives.)

Ministers from the Sturgeon Bay area would assemble groups and visit the area's cherry orchards for the traditional Blessing of the Blossoms during May. The Moravian Church Choir from Sturgeon Bay is shown at one of the local orchards during the 1950s. (Courtesy of Moravian Church of Sturgeon Bay Archives.)

Wayside chapels were built by the Belgian-American community throughout southern Door County since the 1860s. These chapels measured about 8 feet by 10 feet and would be visited at the end of a day's work. On Ascension Sunday, the Rogation procession from a Belgian-American Catholic church would march along the road to the nearest chapel. The procession was led by a cross-bearer in surplice and cassock, followed by little girls dressed in white. They threw flower petals in the path of the priest who carried the Blessed Sacrament. Over the priest's head was a canopy carried by four men. Choir members followed singing hymns, then the women praying the rosary, and last the men of the congregation. When the procession arrived at the chapel, a benediction was said and the procession returned to the church. As more automobiles began using the roads, the processions were canceled for safety reasons.

The inside of a Belgian wayside chapel usually had an altar, religious pictures, sacred objects, and personal papers such as a baptismal certificate or marriage certificate. Several such chapels remain open in southern Door County.

Members of Sturgeon Bay's St. Joseph Parish are pictured here on the day of their First Holy Communion. Communicants were usually members of the second grade at the parish's school and older members of the community who recently joined the congregation. It is said that all large classes throughout the peninsula were bussed in and "graduated" from St. Joseph, since the steps of the church made it easy for a photographer to photograph a large group with a minimum of preparation. (Courtesy of St. Joseph Parish Archives.)

The Sodality of the Immaculate Conception of the Blessed Virgin Mary was organized in 1886 at the St. Joseph Parish in Sturgeon Bay. One of the activities associated with devotion to Mary during the month of May was the May crowning. This took place in the church the first of May following a procession around the church. The scene above is from the early 1950s. (Courtesy of St. Joseph Parish Archives.)

This is the Confirmation Class of 1919 at the Lutheran Church (present-day Immanuel Lutheran Church) in Baileys Harbor. Although there were no dress requirements, the girls always dressed in white and the boys wore suits. Belts must have been "in," for every boy had a suit with a belted jacket. Youngsters were usually confirmed when they were in the eighth grade. Sometimes brothers and sisters were in the same class, since the period of instruction before the Confirmation was usually between one and three years, with students attending instruction on Saturday for two hours. Most students worked on farms at this time. Instruction in the early history of the church was always in German. However, by 1919 instruction and other church services were in English. The students are, from left to right, as follows: (front row) Gladys Walker, Arnold Ohnesorge, Pastor Sturtz, Arthur Reimer, and Adeline Peil; (back row) Walter Abrahamson, Martha Peil, Elda Oldenberg, Violet Anclam, Otto Zachow, Irene Hanson, Ellen Woldt, Esther Stenzel, and Henry Hickory. (Courtesy of Immanuel Lutheran Church Archives.)

Throughout the years, particularly in earlier days near the turn of the century, the young boys of St. Joseph Parish in Sturgeon Bay were eager to be altar boys. It was always considered a sought-after position even though all prayers had to be memorized in Latin and there were numerous early risings to serve mass. This photo from the 1920s shows the altar boys with the pastor, Rev. Alphonse Broens. (Courtesy of St. Joseph Parish Archives.)

When Alma Lundberg and Proctor Waldo married in the early 1900s in Fish Creek, the Community Church altar, pews, and walls were decorated with flowers and ribbons. The Community Church was the former Fish Creek Baptist Community Church. (Courtesy of Gibraltar Historical Association.)

Brann Brothers Department Store is pictured here in Baileys Harbor near the area where Nelson's Hardware is today. Moritz Weiss Sr. owned the blacksmith shop on the right. Harry Brann was also the town's funeral director and would sell caskets at the store. The photo was taken in 1906, the day of Jacob Brann's funeral. (Courtesy of Allen Erickson.)

This is a funeral procession in 1905 to Shiloh Moravian Church. The Odd Fellows and Woodmen societies marched from Sturgeon Bay to the church on present-day Shiloh Road. The original church was built in 1881 for the congregation at Shiloh. A tornado destroyed that church building in 1885, and another church, the present Shiloh Moravian Church, was built on the same spot and was in use in 1886. (Courtesy of Jim and Eileen Robertson.)

The Andrew Salon Funeral Home of Sturgeon Bay first used a horse-drawn hearse, built in 1913, by the Michigan Hearse and Carriage Company of Grand Rapids, Michigan. In 1925, after Jack Stoneman Sr. purchased the funeral business, the hearse was used by the Stoneman Funeral Home until 1927. The hearse was moved to the Oconto Falls area around 1970, when the Soulek Funeral Home, the predecessor of the present Forbes Funeral Home, took over ownership of the funeral business. The hearse was returned to the Sturgeon Bay area in 1982, thanks to the efforts of Sturgeon Bay resident Gary K. Soule, and is on display at the Door County Historical Museum. The hearse is 13 feet long; 5 feet, 8 inches wide; and 7 feet, 3 inches high. Norbert Schulties was the driver of the hearse when it appeared in a Sturgeon Bay parade. (Courtesy of Forbes Funeral Home.)

Five

EDUCATION

The oldest schoolhouse in Door County was built as a result of a meeting on December 7, 1865. The school district, which included Sister Bay, Appleport, Rowleys Bay, and Wildwood, was organized on that date. The first year's budget was $200. The log-cabin schoolhouse was built just north of today's Sister Bay, and classes were conducted until 1881. The building was used for private purposes but was deteriorating during the 1960s when it was deeded to the Door County Historical Society. It was restored as a Bicentennial project and dedicated October 17, 1976, in Gateway Park at the intersection of Highways 42 and 57, where it serves as a tourist information center at the present time.

The Pioneer School House above Ephraim was built in 1880. It was half the size of the building standing today. Cordelia Burt, the first teacher at this school, taught 33 students in grades one through eight in one room. The Pioneer School House was closed in 1949, and the school was preserved for the community at that time after the Ephraim Foundation was formed. The school is now open to the public.

Children from District School House Number Three are pictured here. That schoolhouse was previously located along Shore Road, south of the Tennison Bay Campground, during the late 1800s, in an area that was later to become the Peninsula State Park at Fish Creek. (Courtesy of Peninsula State Park Archives.)

Jacksonport's first schoolhouse was probably built in 1869. The second schoolhouse, shown above, was completed between 1878 and 1880. It was used both as a one-room schoolhouse and as a graded schoolhouse. Albert Edward Halstead was one of the school's early principals since "he was big enough to handle the kids." After he graduated from Sturgeon Bay High School in 1885 in a class of two, he went on to the University of Wisconsin and Northwestern Medical School, where he earned a medical degree. Around 1890 the school was declared a Wisconsin Teacher's Institute for a summer session, and eighth grade graduates were prepared to become teachers. Students who attended and completed the summer session were given teaching certificates from the State of Wisconsin. (Courtesy of James Halstead Sr. and the Jacksonport Historical Society.)

The Jacksonport elementary school is pictured here around 1930. In 1932, after it was state graded, it was to be considered a two-room schoolhouse. When this building opened in 1930, it had about 50 students in one room with all eight grades. Gertrude Matcek, the first teacher, taught all eight grades. Each class was allotted about 15 minutes. Since the first and second graders heard all the lessons for six or seven years, it was said that each graduating class was "getting smarter." There was emphasis on penmanship in all classes, and agriculture was taught in eighth grade. (Courtesy of James Halstead Sr. and the Jacksonport Historical Society.)

Guardian Angel School, seen here in 1896, was established by St. Joseph Parish in Sturgeon Bay. The school opened October 2, 1888, with four grades, one through four. A grade was added every year for the following four years. (Courtesy of St. Joseph Parish Archives.)

Here is the second graduating class of the Holy Guardian Angel School at St. Joseph Parish in Sturgeon Bay in 1895. The first graduating class, the year before, had no boys. Most boys were needed to work on the farm, and many did not graduate from schools until well into the 20th century. (Courtesy of St. Joseph Parish Archives.)

The graduating class of Sturgeon Bay's St. Joseph Parish in 1924 still reflects an overwhelming majority of girls. (Courtesy of St. Joseph Parish Archives.)

The Guardian Angel School at St. Joseph Parish had as many as 77 students in one class, such as Sister Othelia's in 1917. Both Dominican and Franciscan Sisters taught at the school over the years. The school population has been in a steady decline since the 1950s, when the population was around 400 (without a kindergarten), to 102 students in 1998 (with a kindergarten). (Courtesy of St. Joseph Parish Archives.)

In 1921 Frederick Victor Poole, third from the left, of the School of the Art Institute of Chicago and Frederick De Forest Schook, also from the Art Institute, began summer art classes for veterans of World War I in an area south of Baileys Harbor. The school was formally conducted for four summers. Sessions were 12 weeks long. Poole continued to visit the area painting and teaching until 1936, when he passed away. The area is sometimes referred to as "Frogtown." Many of the veterans associated their memories of French soldiers, whom they called "froggies" because of their dress, with the lifestyle that developed at the art school.

Bjorklunden Vid Sjorn ("birch forest by the water") was the summer home of the late Donald and Winifred Boynton of Highland Park, Illinois. It is located about 1 mile south of Baileys Harbor. The chapel on the grounds was handcrafted by the Boyntons between 1939 and 1947. The ornate carving and 41 hand-painted murals are the chapel's most distinctive features. The chapel and the 405-acre estate were bequeathed to Lawrence University in 1963, which conducts seminars and other educational programs on the grounds at the present time. (Courtesy of John Enigl.)

Six
RESORTS

The Nicolet Bay area along Green Bay in Peninsula State Park is pictured here around 1900. Today the same area is a busy beach and may have well over 200 boats rafted on a busy weekend. (Courtesy of Peninsula State Park Archives.)

Originally built as a homestead during the 1860s, the beams that were used in the original construction of this building are still in place. The first public use of the building was as the Central Hotel, later known as Barringer's, in Fish Creek. It could provide for 50 guests. During the 1920s it was converted into makeshift boarding facilities for the high school students from Washington Island and other areas attending Gibraltar High School. Afterwards, it was owned by Dick Wiesgerber of the Green Bay Packers (who now owns a restaurant in Baileys Harbor), and today it is operated as the C and C Supper Club. (Courtesy of Peninsula State Park Archives.)

This is the old Thorp bathhouse in the early years of the 20th century. The Welcker Resort Casino, today's Whistling Swan, is on the left. To the immediate left of the bathhouse is the area of today's Fish Creek Beach. (Courtesy of Gibraltar Historical Association.)

The Maple Tree Cafe is shown here in early Fish Creek. Matt Reilly of Chicago was the architect when it was built in 1910. For several years it served only desserts to the many vacationers in the area. The cafe also hosted bridge parties for the guests of Welcker's Casino and the Thorp Hotel. The interior was made of southern pine, which was never finished or covered. The former Maple Tree Cafe is today's Summertime Restaurant. (Courtesy of Gibraltar Historical Association.)

The Nook Hotel, as it appeared around 1910 in Fish Creek, is on the left. In the center is the personal residence of Henry Duclon, who lived there with his wife, Julia, and eight sons. Duclon was the retired lighthouse keeper from the Eagle Lighthouse in Peninsula State Park. (Courtesy of Gibraltar Historical Association.)

The Liberty Grove Hotel in Sister Bay was opened in 1894 by John and Mary Worachek. The first floor had a large room for dancing and card playing, a lounge, dining room, and kitchen. There were 13 rooms on the second floor which remained open throughout the year. There were also outhouses, a changing cabana for bathers, a wash house, an ice shed, and a small pier. The daughters of the owners and several other girls reportedly formed Sister Bay's first basketball team, playing their games in the hotel's dance hall. Formerly the site of the Hub's Motel and Pier, the area will reopen as Heritage Habor Waterfront Residences. (Courtesy of Allen Erickson.)

Liberty Park Summer Resort, which opened in 1898 in Sister Bay, Wisconsin, was a favorite stop for passengers who traveled on the Goodrich Boats that toured throughout the area for several decades. After guests arrived at Abraham A. Carlson's resort, there was croquet, badminton, ping pong, horseshoes, and tennis. Guests could also fish or play cards. In the early 1900s Liberty Park guests were on the American Plan—three full-course meals were provided with plenty of snacks. The ice in the tea was from the ice stored, since the previous winter, in the icehouse in back of the resort. (Courtesy of Allen Erickson.)

This is Dr. Fickner's "Forest Ideal" retirement home in Sister Bay in the early years of the 20th century. Later uses of the building were as a restaurant and as a nursing home managed by Mr. and Mrs. Irwin Bastian. The building occupied the area behind today's St. Rosalia Church and was near the bluff overlooking Green Bay. (Courtesy of Allen Erickson.)

The Evergreen Beach Hotel in Ephraim opened in 1897. It was built by Fordel Hogenson, who also built his own schooner, *Ebenezer*, and with it hauled enough lumber from Menominee, Michigan, to build the hotel. The hotel had three floors and a porch that surrounded the entire building. There were 22 bedrooms. Room and board for a week cost $5 per person. During the 1930s a large bathroom was added on the second floor, and separate bathrooms were built on the third floor for men and women. Use of the tub, with water brought up after being heated on the kitchen stove on the first floor, added an additional charge of 25¢ to the guest's bill. (Courtesy of Allen Erickson.)

The Anderson Hotel, in the center, is pictured here during the 1920s. The steps in the center background replaced a laundry that was in that area a few years earlier. The Ephraim Moravian church is on the right. (Courtesy of Mary Wilson.)

A resort known as The Cove was opened in Sturgeon Bay around 1900. It, and many other resorts, were built after a fire destroyed the popular Idlewild Resort, which opened in 1897. The Cove was able to accommodate 200 guests. Resorts catered to specific interests. The Pines at Idlewild was a hunting lodge accommodating up to 100 guests. Cabot's Lodge at Idlewild had room for 250 guests. It was built on the exact spot where the first summer resort was built in Door County in 1879 by J.T. Wright. The Happy Hour Resort specialized in fishing and camping trips. The Bay Shore Inn, after it opened in 1922, attracted notable guests such as "Red" Smith, a writer for the *New York Times* who often mentioned the Bay Shore in his sports columns.

On LAKE MICHIGAN and GREEN BAY

TOURIST ROUTES and RATES

VIA LAKE and RAIL

Meals and berth included in rate where star (★) is shown.

To AGENTS:—In drawing orders for tickets via routes shown below, do not fail to show route number and rate from Chicago on order. Special routes and rates furnished on application.

R. C. DAVIS, Gen. Pass. Agt., Foot Michigan Ave., Chicago.

Local Passenger Fares	From Chicago		From Milwaukee	
	One Way	Round Trip	One Way	Round Trip
Chicago . . . . .Ill.	. . . .	. . . .	$ 1.00	$ 1.50
Ephraim . . . . .Wis.	★ $8.00	★ $15.00	★ 7.00	★13.00
Escanaba . . . . .Mich.	★ 8.00	★ 15.00	★ 7.00	★13.00
Fish Creek . . . . .Wis.	★ 8.00	★ 15.00	★ 7.00	★13.00
Green Bay . . . . .Wis.	★ 8.00	★ 15.00	★ 7.00	★13.00
Grand Haven . . . . .Mich.	1.50	2.75	. . . .	. . . .
Grand Rapids . . . . .Mich.	2 00	3 75	. . . .	. . . .
Kewaunee . . . . .Wis.	3.25	5.50	2.25	4.00
Lake Harbor (Hotel). . .Mich.	Sell to Muskegon			
Mackinac Island . . . . . .Mich.	★ 10.00	★ 18.00	★ 10.00	★18.00
Manitowoc . . . . .Wis.	2.25	3.75	1.25	2.25
Marinette . . . . .Wis.	★ 8.00	★ 15.00	7.00	★13.00
Menominee . . . . .Mich.	★ 8.00	★ 15.00	7.00	★13.00
Milwaukee . . . . .Wis.	1.00	1.50	. . . .	. . . .
Milwaukee { Good only on S. S. "Columbus," going and returning same day.	. . . .	1.00	. . . .	. . . .
Muskegon . . . . .Mich.	1.50	2.75	. . . .	. . . .
Racine . . . . .Wis.	1.00	1 50	.25	.50
Sheboygan . . . . .Wis.	2.00	3.25	1.00	1.75
Sister Bay . . . . .Wis.	★ 8.00	★ 15.00	★ 7.00	★13.00
Sturgeon Bay . . . . .Wis.	★ 6.50	★ 12.00	★ 5.00	★ 9.50
Washington Island . . . . .Wis.	★ 8.00	★ 15.00	★ 7.00	★13.00
White Hall (White Lake)Mich.	1.75	3.00	. . . .	. . . .

ROUTE 1.   { ★ Goodrich Transit Co. . . . . . . .to Mackinac Island
Buffalo   Detroit & Cleveland Nav. Co..to Detroit
New York   Detroit & Buffalo S. B. Co..to Buffalo
     From Chicago or Milwaukee, $18.00.
     Round Trip $32.50

The schedules for Goodrich Boats on Lake Michigan and Green Bay tourist routes and rates are pictured here. (Courtesy of Gibraltar Bay Historical Association.)

Goodrich Boat Day on Washington Island usually meant a boat such as the *Carolina* arriving at the Furlong dock. Until about 1920, one ship such as the *Carolina* would regularly dock at Washington Island. In 1923 the regular route of the *Carolina*, when it traveled between Chicago and Mackinac Island, included stops at Sturgeon Bay, Fish Creek, Ephraim, Sister Bay, and Washington Island. In 1924, after Goodrich merged with the Morton Line, three ships per week were traveling to Door County. By the late 1920s the line began reporting financial losses. (Courtesy of Dick Purinton.)

This photo shows the steamer *Georgia* at Anderson's Dock in Ephraim, Wisconsin, around 1910. (Courtesy of Allen Erickson.)

The *City of Luddington*, a Goodrich boat, stops in Sturgeon Bay around 1920. The Goodrich Line used distinctive features and sounds so that its ships could be easily identified. Some had red smokestacks with an orange cast and a broad, black band. Their whistles were usually a melodious tone. The Goodrich dock in Sturgeon Bay later became a dock used by Peterson Builders. When Sturgeon Bay froze, passengers would unload at Lily Bay, and horse-drawn sleighs would transport them to Sturgeon Bay. (Original photography by W.C. Schroeder; courtesy of Roger Schroeder.)

A Goodrich boat is arriving at Ephraim, Wisconsin. The date was the early 1920s. By the mid-1920s almost all ships traveling to the Door peninsula had converted from wood and coal burning, which emitted heavy black smoke, to oil, which was a cleaner fuel. The Goodrich Line always attempted to maintain high standards of cleanliness, service, and courtesy. (Courtesy of Mary Wilson.)

Lovers Leap projected and hung over the water near the Sherwood Point Lighthouse in Sturgeon Bay. It was a popular tourist and picnic destination during the first decade of the 20th century. Thousands of names were etched on the rocks. Early one morning in August 1912 (although the date is in dispute), the rock crashed into the water. There were no reported injuries.

The Adventure Island Camp, established in 1925 on one of the Strawberry Islands between Chambers Island and Ephraim, attracted boys between 7 and 11 years old. The founder and "Skipper" was Charles Kinney. He taught sailing and frequently would stage pageants and other festivities on the water using his Viking ship called "Serpent of the Sea." The camp had a difficult time surviving during the Depression. A severe storm wrecked the camp pier, which further added to the burden of upkeep. The camp eventually closed in the early 1950s. (Courtesy of Mary Wilson.)

There are more than a dozen caves in Door County. The most famous is the cave in Eagle Cliff at the Peninsula State Park. It measures some 42 feet in length and was a popular tourist attraction during the 1920s, when a stairway was built to its entrance. Today the cave is closed to pedestrian traffic. Other caves in Door County include the Horseshoe Bay Cave, which was discovered in 1879. It is the longest cave in Wisconsin, measuring 3,103 feet. It would involve a 13-hour trip to fully explore it. The deepest Wisconsin cave is the Brussels Pit Cave in southern Door County; it measures some 92 feet.

Vacationers were brought to Fish Creek in specially-designed car vans during the 1920s. Most streets were still dirt at the time, with a few made from cobblestone. The Lundbergh Store and the Hill Store are seen in the background. (Courtesy of Gibraltar Historical Association.)

Maxwelton Braes Golf Course and Resort, 1 mile south of Baileys Harbor, was opened May 27, 1931. It was built by Michael W. McArdle, a native of Baileys Harbor who became a successful businessman in Chicago, on land his parents had owned since 1871. Each guest room had a telephone and bath, which, at the time, was considered luxurious. The golf course was designed by Joseph R. Roseman of Chicago. When the course opened, it had 72 traps and was considered quite challenging. As business increased, par was reduced to 70 from 72, and there were 12 fewer traps on the 6,070-yard course. Over the years noted personalities, such as comedian Bob Hope and presidential candidate Thomas E. Dewey, were frequent and regular guests.

After finishing 18 holes at Maxwelton Braes, golfers were invited to take a shot at the course's 19th hole. The hole was 60 yards long with a green 18 feet across. Only a pitched shot had a chance to stay on the green, since the front of the hole was guarded by a sand trap. Players making the shot were rewarded with a gold-bronze medal indicating a hole-in-one. As the player making the hole-in-one approached the 19th green, the medal was being prepared for the golfer. The lucky ball traveled through a mechanism which automatically released the medal with the golfer's ball. The 19th hole was discontinued in the early 1950s. (Courtesy of Maxwelton Braes.)

"Big" Bill Thompson, mayor of Chicago, owned a yacht which he frequently traveled on to visit the waters around Washington Island. Thompson had a cabin, purchased in 1910, on Chester Hjortur Thordarson's property on Rock Island. Thordarson bought the entire island, with the exception of the federally owned lighthouses, around 1900. He developed a collection of some 11,000 rare books and collector's first editions, which he made available to scholars throughout the world. After his death, the collection was donated to the University of Wisconsin. (Courtesy of Washington Island Archives.)

Fred Hotz Sr., known as the "Diamond King," is pictured here on Champagne Rock around 1900. This rock, on which many have since posed, was at the end of Cottage Row in Fish Creek. A successful businessman, Hotz purchased and set aside a large amount of land in the Fish Creek area to keep it from being harvested for lumber. (Courtesy of Gibraltar Historical Association.)

Kangaroo Lake is a 1,100-acre lake located about 2 miles southwest of Baileys Harbor. The lake was named "Kangaroo" since its shape resembles that of a kangaroo. The area remained rather isolated even after a bridge was built across the lake in the 1890s. The bridge could not support teams of horses or automobiles. In the 1920s individual lots were sold along the lake, and some cottages were built. Discussion developed about building a causeway across the narrow portion of the lake. The project began in 1927 and was completed in 1928. Since there was considerable concern about the effects of the causeway, a Kangaroo Lake Association was organized in 1928 to deal with future potential problems. (Courtesy of Allen Erickson.)

A ski jump was developed in Peninsula State Park during the 1930s to attract winter vacationers. The jump was removed after a few years since there were not many experienced jumpers using the facility. (Original photography by W.C. Schroeder; courtesy of Roger Schroeder.)

Seven

CULTURAL AND SOCIAL LIFE

The preservation of tradition was evident in numerous festivities throughout Door County's history. The Fourth of July parades have been taking place in Baileys Harbor since 1891. This wagon in a parade in Baileys Harbor in 1910 featured the Baileys Harbor Woman's Club, with women wearing their native country's colors. The scene is the main street in front of Smith's Saloon, which later became a grocery store. Baseball, sulky races, and bicycle races were featured. "Exotic" foods were sometimes introduced during these events. Anna McArdle came to her first Fourth of July parade in 1896, when she was six years old. Her brother bought her the first banana she ever saw and ate. An annual Fourth of July parade still marches down Baileys Harbor Main Street every year. (Courtesy of Jeanette McArdle.)

This parade on Cedar Street, today's Third Avenue, in downtown Sturgeon Bay was probably for a Fourth of July observance. Fourth of July parades have been very popular throughout the Door peninsula and still take place in several villages today. (Courtesy of Door County Museum.)

At the urging of Hjalmar Rued Holand, an early historian of the Door peninsula, a monument was built honoring the Native Americans of the Door peninsula. Holand suggested a totem pole which symbolized the religion, myths, and life of the Potawatomi Indians and their friendliness to the white people. The pole, made from a 40-foot pine found in the Peninsula State Park, was erected and dedicated on August 14, 1927, on the golf course at the Peninsula State Park. Chief Simon Onanguisse Kahquados, a descendent of the Potawatomi who had a settlement in the Sturgeon Bay area, was present for the dedication. The original began to deteriorate and was replaced with a second pole on July 14, 1970. (Courtesy of Mary Wilson.)

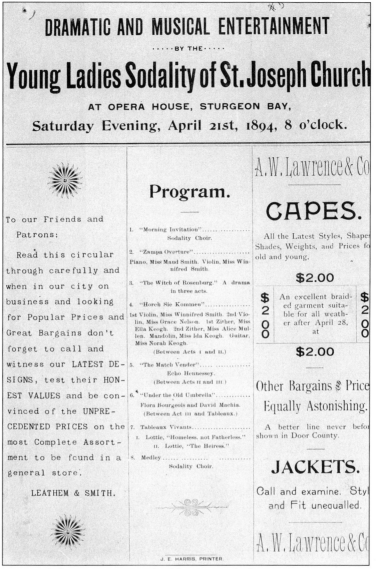

DRAMATIC AND MUSICAL ENTERTAINMENT
·····BY THE·····
Young Ladies Sodality of St. Joseph Church
AT OPERA HOUSE, STURGEON BAY,
Saturday Evening, April 21st, 1894, 8 o'clock.

To our Friends and
  Patrons:

  Read this circular
through carefully and
when in our city on
business and looking
for Popular Prices and
Great Bargains don't
forget to call and
witness our LATEST DE-
SIGNS, test their HON-
EST VALUES and be con-
vinced of the UNPRE-
CEDENTED PRICES on the
most Complete Assort-
ment to be found in a
general store.

    LEATHEM & SMITH.

Program.

1. "Morning Invitation".....................
          Sodality Choir.
2. "Zampa Overture"......................
Piano, Miss Maud Smith. Violin, Miss Win-
          nifred Smith.
3. "The Witch of Rosenburg." A drama
          in three acts.
4. "Horch Sie Kommen"................
1st Violin, Miss Winnifred Smith. 2nd Violin, Miss Grace Nelson. 1st Zither, Miss
Ella Keogh. 2nd Zither, Miss Alice Mul-
len. Mandolin, Miss Ida Keogh. Guitar,
Miss Norah Keogh.
          (Between Acts I and II.)
5. "The Match Vender"....................
          Echo Hennessey.
          (Between Acts II and III.)
6. "Under the Old Umbrella"............
   Flora Bourgeois and David Machia.
          (Between Act III and Tableaux.)
7. Tableaux Vivants.....................
   I. Lottie, "Homeless, not Fatherless."
      II. Lottie, "The Heiress."
8. Medley.......................
          Sodality Choir.

J. E. HARRIS, PRINTER.

A. W. Lawrence & Co

CAPES.

All the Latest Styles, Shapes
Shades, Weights, and Prices fo
old and young,

$2.00

$ 2 0 0	An excellent braid-ed garment suita-ble for all weath-er after April 28, at	$ 2 0 0

$2.00

Other Bargains & Price
Equally Astonishing.

A better line never befor
shown in Door County.

JACKETS.

Call and examine. Styl
and Fit unequalled.

A. W. Lawrence & Co

There is question if there ever was a building named the Sturgeon Bay Opera House. A two-story building was constructed by John Goettelman to house a doctor's residence, his office, and a drugstore. A rear annex was added and named "The Bayview Opera." However, it was used for dances and as a meeting hall. In the first two decades of the 20th century, it was called the "Sawyer Opera House" and was the social and entertainment center of the west side. It also served as the Sawyer Post Office. A few years later it was a roller rink and it showed silent movies. Huge mass meetings gathered there in 1909 when the City abolished its saloons and then reinstated them a year later. Several religious groups in need of temporary facilities met there. The Corpus Christi congregation, interestingly a group which formed within the St. Joseph Parish community, held services in the hall until its own church could be built. The Great Depression closed the "opera" house until 1940, when it was purchased by William and Salina Andre. Sam and Sandy Andre purchased the business in 1987. Today it is known as "Andre's Food and Spirits." There is no record of an opera being performed at either the Bayview or the Sawyer "opera" houses. (Courtesy of St. Joseph Parish Archives.)

The Leonhardt Music Hall was probably one of the "opera houses" in downtown Sturgeon Bay around 1900. The hall was used by various groups who staged musical productions. The building burned down, and its place at 66 South Third Street is now occupied by the Red Room. (Courtesy of the Door County Museum.)

During the 1920s the Ephraim Sunday evening community sings were very popular. They were conducted outdoors or in a church. The need for a permanent location for the popular programs, other community activities, and village meetings became apparent. William C. Bernhard, a summer resident and architect from Chicago, promoted the idea of a village hall that reflected the Scandinavian heritage of the village. Bernhard, who was selected as the architect for the Village Hall, had designed the summer home of Frederick Stock, director of the Chicago Symphony Orchestra, in Ephraim. Fred Crandall, an architect from Sturgeon Bay, was called in to oversee the construction of the center. Limestone from Eagle Bluff was used. In winter, the stone was hauled across the bay on horse-drawn sleighs. The building was completed and opened in the summer of 1927. It has served as the Ephraim Village Hall until the present day. (Courtesy of Mary Wilson.)

The Union Band was especially popular for the many social events in the Belgian-American community of southern Door County in the early 20th century. The "Kermiss," a three-day weekend festival of music, dancing, games, and plenty of food, was observed by each of the church parishes in the area. At the St. Mary of the Snows Church, the Union Band also provided the music for the folk dances performed on the road and known as "dust dances." Belgian folksongs were sung throughout the night. Earlier in the day, games included climbing greased poles, catching a greased pig, and blindfolding men who then attempted to decapitate a goose with a scythe. (Courtesy of Harry Chaudoir Sr.)

When Ester Evrard and Charles Bader were married in 1909, the entire parish community of St. Mary of the Snows Church in southern Door County was invited. The Union Band, lower left, provided the entertainment. (Courtesy of Harry Chaudoir Sr.)

Harriet Maples Dier, wife of the Sturgeon Bay Canal master, is at the piano for a family sing-along. The photo was probably taken between 1890 and 1900. (Courtesy of Joanne M. Mathes and Door County Maritime Museum.)

Every weekend Winona Young and her orchestra provided the entertainment for the dances at Nelson's Hall on Washington Island. A notice, posted in Mann's store encouraging "Y'all Come," resulted in crowds of up to 150 or more. The group also performed at private birthday parties, wedding receptions, and other personal affairs. The group was popular during the 1920s and 1930s when the above photo was taken (1928). (Courtesy of Washington Island Archives.)

116

Gabler's Fernwood Garden Tavern was a popular spot for dances in the Jacksonport community. The hall could accommodate as many as 400 dancers and was also used for wedding receptions and other community affairs. During the 1920s and 1930s most who attended had to wait until they could "hitch" a ride with someone who had a car, since many were without transportation. (Courtesy of Jams Halstead Sr. and the Jacksonport Historical Society.)

Nightly entertainment was provided at the Peninsula State Park near Fish Creek in the Huber Theater in the Weborg Point Campground. The above photo was taken around 1935. (Courtesy of Peninsula State Park Archives.)

The kitchen crew was active during the dedication ceremonies of Lakeside Park in Jacksonport, September 3, 1939, preparing an all-day hot dog stand and coffee for 1,000 guests. It was the town's first park and occupied a little over an acre. The guest speaker for the day was former attorney general John Reynolds, with Grover Stapleton, who later became the county judge, as the master of ceremonies. Working in the kitchen were, from left to right, as follows: Lydia Schmidt, Lucietta Logerquist, Lydia Bley, Martha Spille, Gertie Erskine, and Lottie Halstead. (Courtesy of James Halstead Sr. and the Jacksonport Historical Society.)

John Goettleman and Pola Emill are at one of the popular bars in Sawyer (Sturgeon Bay) around 1900. The bar, open every day, served many of the workers from Leathem and Smith who lived upstairs in the lodgings provided by the Bay View House. Beer was 5¢ for a large stein. Plenty of tobacco must have been chewed, since no one was ever more than a few feet away from a spittoon. (Courtesy of Goettleman family collections.)

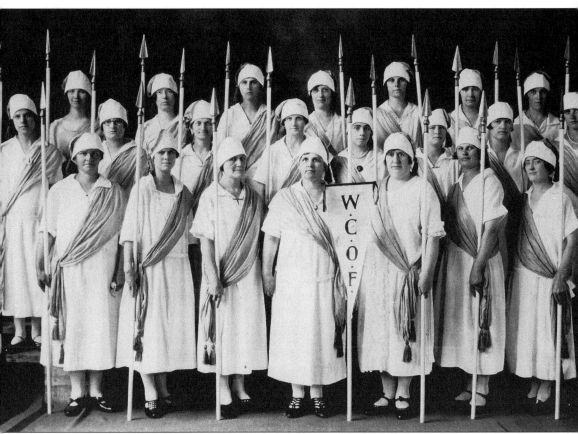

The Women's Catholic Order of Foresters, a fraternal benefit society, was organized at St. Joseph Parish in Sturgeon Bay around 1900. All members wore uniforms and would follow strict ritualistic practices. They would march in unison into the hall where meetings were conducted in full uniform. The meetings in Sturgeon Bay were conducted above Moeller's Garage. No definitive explanation could be verified explaining the purpose of the spears. Some believe it symbolized preparedness to defend the Catholic faith. Pat DeNys, of the National Catholic Society of Foresters, successor to the Woman's Catholic Order of Foresters, says that sashes similar to those above are still worn today, but other elements of the garb are no longer in use. (Courtesy of St. Joseph Parish Archives.)

After the first Good Templar's Lodge burned down, a second was built in 1887. The Good Templars advocated abstinence from all alcoholic beverages. They used the hall for dances that went well into the night. They also sponsored many parades. After World War I the front of the building was used as a town hall and the rear was used for veterans of World War I. A Community Club also used the facilities to stage theatrical productions, host guest speakers, and conduct other programs. The school staged its Christmas plays at the hall. Another recent use for the town hall was as a bakery. (Courtesy of James Halstead Sr. and the Jacksonport Historical Society.)

Wood choppers are shown here in the Sturgeon Bay area. The photo was taken in 1889. The "M" and "W" on the sweaters suggests the group is a lodge or fraternal benefit society of the Modern Woodmen or the Woodmen and the Mystic Works, both active in the area at the time. The workers have been identified as (from left to right): (sitting in front or not pictured) Benny Gerard, Fred Wilkes, William Fields, Matt Dier, John Walker, Melvin Austin, and Joseph Bunda; (center with sweaters) Dick Walker, Henry Klessing, Pete George, and John Walker; (back row) Gus Johnson, Joe Stoffels, Joe Sucky, Hans Zettle, Frank Lauscher, Chas Felhofer, Hans Nelson, Geo Fields, and Ted Maples. (Courtesy of the Door County Museum.)

Aslag Anderson came to Ephraim in 1856, bought 300 acres of land, farmed, and constructed a store and a pier. Anderson's store became the center of business in Ephraim for over 100 years. The Andersons had 13 children, 10 of whom lived to be adults. Over the years the Anderson family has continued to enjoy family gatherings in the backyard of the family home in Ephraim. The gentleman fourth from the left is Adolf Anderson, son of Aslag and grandfather of Henry A. Anderson, M.D., of Madison, Wisconsin. The above photo was taken around 1890. (Courtesy of Henry A. Anderson, M.D.)

Christmas is celebrated at the home of the superintendent of the Sturgeon Bay Canal, Adam Norman Dier, around 1900. The adults are probably Adam Norman Dier and his wife, Harriet (Maples) Dier. (Courtesy of Joanne M. Mathes and Door County Maritime Museum.)

What was probably a gentlemen's bicycle club is on an outing on Washington Island during the 1920s. The formal dress—all but one man is sporting a tie—suggests they may have been visiting one of the exclusive camps on the island, such as Camp Pan Hellenic, where the young ladies dressed in uniforms for many of their outings and activities. (Courtesy of Washington Island Archives.)

Young ladies in their Sunday best enjoy an outing at Cape Point near Baileys Harbor around 1900. (Courtesy of Gloria Hansen.)

The Jacksonport baseball team is pictured in 1915 when it played regular games against teams from Egg Harbor, Baileys Harbor, and Washington Island. Fred Erskine (first row, extreme left) purchased a Sears Roebuck camera in 1910 and became quite a noted photographer in Jacksonport. He probably took the above photo with a remote system, frequently used, to insure he would be in the photo. After Erskine took the photos, he would develop the print using glass negatives. In 1960 Sears recognized Erskine as one of the first purchasers of this camera. It is reported that the camera was still operational in 1998. (Courtesy of James Halstead Sr. and the Jacksonport Historical Society.)

A baseball game was usually one of the attractions for the Fourth of July observances in Baileys Harbor. This game was played in 1920 in a field that is now occupied by the Associated Bank, Baileys Harbor Cinema, and Wiesgerber's Pub. (Courtesy of Immanuel Lutheran Church Archives.)

The Ephraim Regatta is an annual summer event that has attracted thousands of viewers and hundreds of participants. In the early years the regatta featured canoe races, canoe tiltings, rowboat races, and tub races. There were also diving and swimming contests. However, since the 1930s, the Ephraim Yacht Club, which was launched in 1906, began to encourage owners of sailboats to participate. The "Flying Scots" have been featured for many years. As one writer has observed, "There will always be an Ephraim regatta." (Courtesy of Mary Wilson.)

The 3,000-yard golf course at Peninsula State Park, built in 1921, was one of the longest in the state of Wisconsin at the time. The course was probably managed by the Ephraim Men's Club in its early days. The course was considered very successful and expanded to 18 holes by the end of the decade. The average number of players on the course on a daily basis had risen to 85 by that time. In 1997 there were 65,000 rounds of nine-hole golf recorded at Peninsula State Park. (Courtesy of Peninsula State Park Archives.)

Rev. Vanden Elsen arrived at St. Mary of the Snow Church in 1919 in his Ford pickup truck, hauling a piano. That vehicle and the "new car" the Reverend purchased a few years later were always an attraction for the young people of the church. Ready to go for a ride are Desire Gerondale, Hermine Gerondale, Emma Gerondale, Lucy LeRoy and her sister, Homer LeRoy, Josie Conrad, Frank DeKeyser, Yevonne Baudhuin, Gabe Gerondale, Lema Charles, and Lema Fontaine. (Courtesy of Harry Chaudoir Sr.)

Belgian ovens were commonly used by the Belgian-American community throughout southern Door County for about 100 years from the mid-19th century. When a festival or other celebration was planned, the Belgian ovens would be fired up and as many as 25 loaves of bread or a dozen pies could be baked at one time. The oven shown above can be seen on the north side of Highway 57 near Namur.

The Belgian community grew rapidly during the 1860s. It was estimated that 15,000 Belgians were living in northeastern Wisconsin at that time. A normal schedule for Belgians was eating five meals a day. There were also many festivals with plenty of food. Belgians were able to prepare large amounts of food in their Belgian ovens. In this photo Reggie Baudhuin seems to anticipate the taste of hot, freshly-baked Belgian bread. (Courtesy of Martha and Reggie Baudhuin.)

Belgian ovens were made of brick. Cedar wood was usually used to fire up the oven since hard wood would make and keep the bricks too hot for baking. This oven near Namur on Highway 57 was built around 1869. Although it could fit as many as 25 loaves of bread or pies, it was usually used once a week during summer to prepare 12 loaves of bread and 12 pies. It was not used in the winter, when baking was done in the home. The oven has seen occasional use the past few years and, if need be, the current owner says, "still can be fired up." (Courtesy of Martha and Reggie Baudhuin.)

The Cupola House in Egg Harbor was planned for ten years. It was completed with 14 rooms, including a large ballroom on the second floor, in 1871. Levi Thorp, the builder, made numerous trips to Menominee, Michigan, across Green Bay to personally select all the wood that would be used in the structure. Thorp rejected lumber that had a knot or any other type of blemish. The Cupola House has been completely restored and is listed in the National Register of Historic Places. It presently serves as a commercial business and is open to the public. (Courtesy of Gloria Hansen.)

This was the personal residence of Herbert C. Scofield, mayor of Sturgeon Bay from 1899 to 1901. The residence, completed in 1902, took two years to build. A specially-designed cistern on the third floor collected rainwater for drinking. The street at the time was named Lawrence; it was changed to, and still is called, Michigan. The sidewalks were wooden. Taxes for the first year on the residence were $13.18. The barn on the right belonged to the Reynolds family orchards. Today the former Scofield residence serves as a bed and breakfast inn. (Courtesy of Bill and Fran Cecil.)

Today's White Lace Inn in Sturgeon Bay, a Queen Anne Victorian–style homestead, was built in 1903 as the personal homestead of Richard P. Cody. Cody was a successful lawyer, district attorney, president, vice-president, and attorney of the Bank of Sturgeon Bay. The second floor had a large meeting room which was used by the Knights of Columbus for about 30 years. The house was renovated in 1982 and is now used as a bed and breakfast inn.

The Adolph Larson building is currently being restored after having been placed on the National Historic Register. Larson was the first cabinet maker in Door County and was known for his original ornamental wood carvings and designs, which have been preserved in the building. The Larson building is regarded as a classic design during the frontier "boomtown" period in Sturgeon Bay. The original Larson building was constructed in 1867.